Too Much Information

Did I really say that?

A collection of humor columns

Lois Swagerty

Volume 1

To Susan
with love ~
Always
keep
laughing :)
♥ Lois Swagerty

DEDICATION

To Mr. Right:

Sexiness wears thin and beauty fades,

But to be married to a man who makes you laugh every day,

Ah, now that's a real treat.

—Joanne Woodward

ACKNOWLEDGMENTS

Thanks to my husband, who has used me in sermon illustrations for the last 30 years. I don't get mad, I get even.

Thanks to my daughter, who says that anything funny I ever wrote, I ripped off from her.

Thanks to Son One, who has become a writer, and Son Two, who always grabbed a paper and read my column. Thanks to my two daughters-in-law who have enriched our family exponentially.

Thanks to Eva Shaw who inspired me to take up writing and sent me to the head of the class.

Thanks to Pat Detmer who suggested that I start with the newspaper in my own driveway.

Thanks to Adam Ward at *Today's Local News* who accepted my first column and asked for more.

Thanks to Lou Bruno at Bruno Advertising+Design who shared his expertise as creative director of this book.

Thanks to Susan Caldwell who designed the cover.

Thanks to all the friends who laughed at my stories, and apologies to those who were afraid to say anything for fear it would show up in print.

INTRODUCTION

Welcome to my world. It's a little twisted, but nobody ever said it'd be safe. There is no known vaccine for over-sharing, only the cringing of my family and the laughter of my friends to egg me on.

I recommend that you take these essays in small doses. When I was small my mother told me never to wear out my welcome, and the same holds true for this book. Always quit reading while you still want more. It's the perfect bathroom book, so be sure to get a copy for each one in your house.

These essays first appeared as weekly columns in *Today's Local News* in Carlsbad, California from 2006–2009. After the paper died (not my fault) I moved online to www.loisswagerty.com where entire years may pass without a new blog post. You can see how the weekly deadlines were the only thing holding my life together.

In the interest of family privacy, the names have been changed to protect the innocent. My offspring will be known as Son One, Son Two, Favorite Dotter and my husband, Mr. Right. If you want to call *me* something else, I'll settle for L'Erma in honor of my patron saint, Erma Bombeck.

As Brett Lott once said, "I am the fool at the center of my own life." By laughing along with me, I hope you will find the humor in your own world.

After all, if you can't laugh at yourself, who *can* you laugh at?

~Lois Swagerty, Fall 2014 ▼

CONTENTS

PART FOUR: Spring

PART FIVE: Summer Again

PART ONE

Summer

.

SWEATING THE SMALL STUFF

FINALLY MY LIFE has value. Like a stamped ticket stub from the parking garage, I feel strangely validated as a mom.

After living more than 20 years in Carlsbad, California with my husband and three kids, I'm taking a look at how they turned out—the kids, that is. Maybe I've made an impact after all.

Recently my oldest son, who lives and works in Los Angeles, turned 23. When I complimented him on spreading his birthday festivities out over two weekends, he said, "I learned it from the best."

He was referring to my talent for making my birthday last as long as possible. Not one to burden any single friend unduly, I collect several cohorts who like to go to the movies, then call in all my chips once a year in a sustained movie-going marathon that lasts for at least a month.

Not to mention last year, when I turned 50, and managed to stretch out the celebration for a record-breaking 50 weeks.

I can't tell you how gratifying it was to hear Son One's words. After years of feeling as if the kids learned absolutely nothing from my efforts at good parenting, the lasting lessons are finally coming home to roost.

Maybe my focus has been wrong. I was looking for eternal values to impart to my offspring. And all along they've been absorbing the small stuff.

Take my 19-year-old daughter, for instance. In her worst nightmare she never wanted to be compared to me, let alone follow in my footsteps. However, last time she was at the chiropractor, she asked for a red pen to jot down the next appointment in her purse calendar.

"Aha!" said the receptionist, "You're just like your mom. She always writes hers in red."

You could hear the reaction for miles. "You've *ruined* me, Mom," she wailed over the phone. "I'm just *like* you. My calendar is *color coded.*"

Personally, I can think of lots worse things about me to emulate. There's my secret obsession of going through the car wash. All those colored, sudsy bubbles massaged over the windshield with rubbery fingers—it doesn't get much better than that.

Unless you count the thwap-thwap-thwap of the side brushes propelling you through, and the sharp scent of soap wafting through the air-conditioning vents. While simultaneously eating chocolate. Who knows, maybe I've passed on this addiction to my daughter as well.

But recently I had the biggest payoff of all. Son Two, who's 21 and spending a semester abroad with an international studies program, called long distance from Spain at the crack of dawn.

"Hey, Mom," he began in a matter-of-fact voice. "I've been arrested. Can you send money to bail me out?"

Why was I so thrilled? Because his next words were music to my ears.

"April Fools!"

My favorite day of the year, and he remembered.

No more regrets about wasted lessons and spurned values for me. This Mother's Day was spent resting on my laurels and patting myself on the back for a job well done. ▼

WARNINGS MAY BE HAZARDOUS TO YOUR HEALTH

LATELY I'VE BEEN paying closer attention to the warnings printed on product labels.

Everybody knows the famous statement on cigarette packages: "Cigarette smoking may be hazardous to your health."

But have you seen the British version? Bold letters shout from the pack:

"Smoking kills."

"Smoking seriously harms you and others around you."

"Smokers die younger."

"Smoking causes male impotence."

And my personal favorite, "Smoking causes aging of the skin."

We've gotten so used to warnings on medications, we hardly pay attention to the dire list of possible side effects. I figure it's too late to worry about birth defects, so I don't read them any more.

But I admire the clever way they fold up fourteen pages of fine print and fit it into a tiny box along with the product. These are people who could make map folders weep with envy.

Food wrappers are a great place to find disclaimers such as "Phenylketonurics: Contains phenylalanine." Say that three times in a row.

Or, "This product was made in a factory that processes peanuts."

Or the mother of all allergy statements, "Products have been produced on equipment shared with peanuts, tree nuts, milk, eggs, soybeans and wheat."

I'll bet the legal writers won first prize in the Cover-Your-Back-side contest when they crafted that one.

Sometimes I don't take warnings seriously enough. This happened one afternoon when I treated myself to a packet of sugar-free jellybeans. The fine print noted: "Excess consumption may have a laxative effect."

How many jellybeans is excessive? I wondered. Starting with two or three, I gradually nibbled 15 or 20 by the end of the afternoon.

My discovery? A handful of sorbitol-laced jellybeans packs the same punch as a Roto-Rooter.

Stronger than a Fleet Prep Kit and just as effective, I now recommend sugar-free jellybeans to anyone getting ready for a colonoscopy.

Why choke down the salty stuff when you could enjoy a tasty snack food? No gagging necessary—these tasty tidbits are easy to ingest and even easier to expel.

I think the classic health alert appears on the Q-tips box. "Not for use in ears," it declares. "WARNING: If used to clean ears, stroke swab gently around the outer surface of the ear without entering the ear canal. **Do not use swab in ear canal**."

That's about as absurd as a No Chewing sign in a bubble gum factory. People have been using cotton swabs to clean out ears since the beginning of time.

That's one reason I had children—so I could clean out their ears.

And have you ever heard the maxim: "Never put anything smaller than an elbow in your ear"? Who are they trying to kid?

To be truthful, I have a friend who punctured her own ear drum with a Q-tip. But there were extenuating circumstances. She had just gotten her arm out of a cast and was a little too eager to catch up on her personal grooming. Her fine-motor control may have been a little rusty.

I'm on the lookout now for other outrageous warnings. Perhaps I've uncovered a secret society, the Warning Writers of America. Maybe I'll attend their next convention.

I'll be sure to bring along my box of Q-tips. ▼

NIGHTSTAND NIGHTMARES

CREEPING EVER HIGHER, it threatens to take over my half of the bedroom.

The stack of books on my nightstand is raging out of control. I knew I was in trouble when the twin towers of tomes rose up past the bottom of the lampshade on my little reading light. Mr. Right noticed the problem and said, "We need to send you to nightstand camp."

This wasn't an idle threat.

For years my family has said that I should be sent away for various remedial reasons.

The men in the clan always complain about my wimpy spitting skills.

"You spit like a girl," they say, and with good reason, since I *am* a girl, and girls aren't technically supposed to spit. But being an ex-jogger gives me the privilege of indulging in emergency expectoration once in a while. Thus the need for a trip to spit camp.

If this rule held true, I can think of plenty of other camps where I could have sent various family members over the years.

How about cleaning your room camp, or putting dirty dishes in the dishwasher camp? Taking phone messages camp could last all summer and offer refresher sessions the following year.

But I digress.

I'll admit to having a severe reading addiction. One of the first symptoms I can remember appeared at an early age on Saturday mornings when I was supposed to be cleaning my room. I would turn on the vacuum, shut the door, and hunker down behind my bed with a Reader's Digest Condensed book. As if my mom wouldn't notice that the vacuum cleaner shriek wasn't moving.

My voracious appetite for books continues to this day. I start to get the shakes if I get down to the last one on my nightstand and supplies are running low.

For years I stockpiled Reader's Digest Condensed books in my bedroom closet, a kind of personal disaster insurance in case I ever got sick and couldn't get out to the library.

Nowadays my book hoard stands proudly out in the open. Numbering 23 volumes at last count, it contains books I want to read, books I ought to read, books I got for Christmas but haven't read, books people have loaned me, books from the library due next week, and one book I must read for book club by tomorrow—like it or not.

Not one to panic, I am convinced that my current overload is temporary.

Besides, it isn't my fault.

Have you ever noticed how, after waiting three months for half a dozen books on request from the library, they all come at once? Usually it's just after you've picked up a hefty supply the day before. And although there's not a name for this syndrome, it never fails. It's like getting your car washed—a virtual guarantee that it will rain the next day.

For now, I'm steadily working my way through the tottering stacks. One by one, the pile will dwindle until I can reach the switch on my lamp.

Last week I requested a new batch of titles from the library. If they all come at once, I'll need a bigger nightstand. ▼

TEMPTING FATE

MY THREE GROWN children are jumping out of an airplane tomorrow.

No matter that they've tried twice before and it's been cancelled on account of cloudy weather.

No matter that Son One's girlfriend fixes him with an icy glare whenever the subject comes up.

No matter that he claims you are much more likely to die on a Los Angeles freeway than from skydiving.

I admit to going paragliding off Torrey Pines cliffs for my birthday last year, foolishly thinking I could inspire my kids to soar instead of plummet.

Instead I'm afraid I spawned a cycle of one-upsmanship, in which they think they can outdo their mother.

They claim they're not trying to compete. "Come along and do it too," they said, generously inviting me, but not offering to pay.

I'm not a worrier, not the kind of mom who lies awake at night thinking about what could go wrong.

That is, not until last Sunday night.

In an untimely convergence of hormones, caffeine, and anxiety, I spent most of the night trying not to think about all that could go awry.

I tried not to think about the sickening possibilities. Tried not to remember my friend's story of her son's parachute opening with only milliseconds before he would hit the ground.

But then, this morning in the bathroom while drying my hair, I caught a glimpse of my holey underpants. I suddenly realized: What am I thinking? I am tempting fate just as much as they are, for a much cheaper price.

Didn't my mother always say, "Never go out in ripped

underwear, because you might get into an accident"?

If she didn't, then she should have. All the good mothers did.

I do have an underwear retirement program; it's not like I keep them forever. When they pass their expiration date, I buy a new supply.

But the old ones are still so comfy and serviceable, I can't always bear to part with them. So I make myself a deal: when putting on a really ratty pair, I vow to throw them away at the end of the day.

This philosophy usually works. I haven't yet had a car wreck or trip to the hospital on a bad-panties day. On the other hand, I have a friend who had a heart attack and lived to regret his underwear choice that morning. The emergency techs had to cut off his best pair of shorts. And you thought this was just a girl-thing.

It's not only about underwear, it could be socks. The last time I wore a holey sock, I paid an unscheduled visit to a foot-comfort store to buy an insert for some cheap tennis shoes.

The saleslady asked me to take off my shoes, then raised her eyebrows when she saw my torn sock. Chagrined, I slipped off the sock, only to reveal a bandaged toe underneath. Needless to say, I never went back to that store again.

I should have learned my lesson. So why am I wearing my second-string undies today? Guess I'm just taking the ultimate gamble, living on the edge, taking a risk.

I don't know where my kids get it. ▼

DEAR TOOTH FAIRY

THEY SAY THE most lucrative kind of writing is a ransom note. Running a close second was my daughter's correspondence with the tooth fairy.

Penciled in earnest with tongue poking out between teeth, she wrote these priceless gems when she was between the ages of 6 and 11 and slipped them under her pillow. We never corrected her spelling.

"Daer toohc ferre. Ples leve the toohc for me and $100. Not." –6 years old

A recycling theme emerged early on.

"Please leave my tooth for my collection. Thanks."

I always suspected she was taking the recovered teeth over to our neighbor's house and getting paid twice for them—a sort of dental double dipping. You had to admire her entrepreneurial instincts.

Gradually the notes became more demanding.

"Dear Tooth Fary, Please leave the tooth for my tooth collection, and if you can, can I have exstra money cos it was hard to get out." –7 years old

For the next three years, her bottom line was terse and to the point: Show me the money, and leave me the tooth.

"Dear Tooth Fairy, Please leave my tooth for my collection. I should get $1 because it hurts, but if you want to give me more, that's fine with me."

"Dear Tooth Fairy, As usual, please leave my tooth for my collection. Thanx. PS: I'm older so I get more money, right?"

At age 10, the notes got chattier.

"Tooth Fairy, Here is the $1 I owe my dad. Please diliver it to him under his pillow. Oh yeah, also my teeth are here just for proof.

(You don't have to pay me if you don't want to, because it costed a lot to get them pulled.) PS.If you don't take my money, don't pretend that is the money you gave me because I'm two smart for that."

Two smart indeed.

"Tooth Fairy, I hope my dad contacted you like he said he would. I don't know what he told you, but yes, this is a huge tooth! I normally wouldn't ask you this, but may I have a little bit extra so I can buy stuff at my retrete in the mountains with my mom? (If not, that is O.K.) Thanks. Toothless"

"Dear Tooth Fairy, Yup, I lost another tooth. I only have 7 more left. Please leave my tooth in the bag provided, for my collection."

"Dear Tooth Fairy, My doctor says I only have one more tooth to lose, but I think there are really 5 left. Please leave my tooth for my collection. Thanks. (Even more toothless)"

When she was 11, an argument broke out between daughter and husband over the identity of the tooth fairy, resulting in a signed statement by her.

"I understand that my father is not the tooth fairy and I will never accuse him of being the tooth fairy in the future."

I confess I was a little misty-eyed when the era came to an end.

"Tooth Fairy: Last tooth! Since it was my 20th tooth that I lost, could I have $20? Please leave my tooth as usual. Please write me a note."

The reply came: "Dear Brave One, Congratulations on losing your last tooth. I hope you are not disappointed with your reward. I only give $20 for wisdom teeth. It has been fun sneaking into your room all these years.

"You are very lucky to have such a wonderful man for your father. And I think your mother is special too. I will miss you. I hope you have wisdom teeth so I can see you again.

"Signed: Your Special Tooth Fairy" ▼

PUTTING THE FUN IN FUNERAL

I'VE ALWAYS SAID, if you want it done right, do it yourself.

In my opinion, this can apply to occasions when you want things to be done a certain way, but other people may not come through for you.

Folks aren't mind readers, at least nobody in my family is, so I try to state my expectations clearly, concisely, right up-front, telling people what I want for my birthday or Christmas or Mother's Day. I don't believe in leaving such things to chance.

Granted, it takes the element of surprise out of the occasion, but it's easier than swallowing the disappointment of opening up a set of cooking pans when you'd been hoping for a cherry-red beach cruiser bike.

Stay with me for a second. Have you ever noticed how funerals can turn into the best parties? Sure, you're sad about the death of a loved one, but it's so wonderful to visit with everyone else. Like one great big class reunion, where all the people you wished would show up, did.

This line of thought leads me to conclude, why not plan my own funeral? And why not schedule it before I'm gone so I can enjoy it too?

I came up with this idea after my 50th birthday party, during which I opened up the floor for people to tell their favorite stories about me. Except for my daughter, who shared about the humiliating time I was pulled over on my bike for running a red light, most people kept mum.

It takes a funeral to get people to admit how they really feel about you. But by then it's too late. Recall the classic story of Tom Sawyer and Huck Finn arriving at their own funeral just in time to hear how wonderful they'd been and how dearly loved.

Now you may be thinking that I'm a Control Freak with a capital

C.F. Not so. I simply hate to miss out on any good time, especially a party.

As a child I would crack open my bedroom door and jam my ear against the crevice, trying to hear what all the laughter was about in the living room after my bedtime. I remember switching sides when one ear got numb, and making a dive for the bed if I heard footsteps approaching.

To this day, I can't stand to miss any occasion that could be fun. If I have to be absent from my book club, for instance, and find out later that everyone had a great time, then I'm secretly afraid it was because I wasn't there.

But back to the funeral plans. Even with a terminal diagnosis, you never know when your last day on earth will come, so it probably pays to throw a big bash ahead of time just in case.

It should have all the ingredients of a regular party: good food, good music, good friends and family, plus a few little extras such as a professional comedian or funny skits, like on the last night of summer camp.

There could also be a plate-licking contest, something my husband hates for me to do in public.

Hey, if the dessert's that good, why not? Just make sure the plate isn't see-through—that's my only advice.

One obvious drawback is having to do all the work yourself. But perhaps there's a niche market out there for pre-death party planners: Fun Funerals and Festivities, Inc.

If the guests don't like my ideas, I'll just break into a song: "It's my party, I can die if I want to." ▼

HELP FOR THE DECISION IMPAIRED

STAGGERING UNDER AN unwieldy load of ten dress shirts as I exited the mall, I barely made it to my car alive.

I had just finished shopping for Mr. Right's birthday. Unlike me, he does not cooperate by providing a wish list, so there's a lot more guesswork involved. How hard can it be, I thought. I'll just pick up a new shirt for his summer wardrobe.

The thing is, I can never remember whether he likes button-down collars or plain. Blends of 50/50, 65/35 or 100% cotton. Wrinkle-free or stain-free.

So many styles, so little time.

And therein lies the problem: I'm terrible at making decisions.

Calling me indecisive is like calling Donald Trump hairstyle challenged.

When it comes to multiple choices, I'm a failure at finality, a duchess of doubt, a hero of hesitance. Unable even to dial in my vote on "American Idol," I could be a poster girl for the decision impaired.

I know it's a woman's prerogative to change her mind, but with me it's more like a full-time job. Most of the time I can pass for normal, but in certain situations my handicap comes to the fore. A simple trip to 31 Flavors ice cream, for instance, can leave me severely traumatized.

Then there's the annual visit to the eye doctor.

Anyone who wears eyeglasses knows how grueling it can be to answer the rapid-fire barrage of questions as you sit there with the machine jammed against your face.

"Which is better," they ask. "One or two? Two or three? Thirteen or fourteen? Better now, or better now?"

It's a nightmare. And there's always a chance they're trying to fool you by using the same lens twice.

Meanwhile the background turns black, the light dims and brightens, and the letters grow fuzzy away as my vision zooms in and out like a deranged camera on auto focus.

Stumped, I make a timid query of my own.

"By 'better' do you mean clearer or darker? One is smaller and one is fatter."

"I think you're reading too much into the question," my doctor sighs, with a tinge of impatience in his voice.

Another danger zone is in restaurants. When ordering food from among so many menu options, I develop a serious case of mental paralysis.

Once I asked for a taste of rice while trying to decide between a side dish of potato or pilaf. The waiter barely suppressed an eye-roll.

"This isn't Costco," commented my long-suffering husband. "They don't hand out free samples."

"I just wanted to know if it was made with real rice or those fake little pasta bullets," I explained.

At least I stay open to trying new choices.

Mr. Right, on the other hand, likes to return to the same restaurant and order the same thing each time. Come to think of it, maybe that's his way of handling his own decision-making issues.

People like me should never try to get a job that calls for instant judgments. Picture an air traffic controller: "Flight 833 cleared for landing…no, no, I take that back." Or an auctioneer: "Sold…uh, not really." Or an umpire: "Strike 3…I mean ball 3." Can you imagine the mayhem?

In most cases I can get by. Barring restaurants and shopping malls, I do pretty well.

As for Mr. Right's pile of 10 new shirts, chances are good he'll like one or two of them.

Add a case of motor oil, throw in a birthday card, and call me done. ▼

COLOR ME CONFUSED

I USED TO KNOW which colors went together.

Growing up in my little clothing universe, there were really only two categories: neutrals and the rest. The neutrals were black, brown and navy. The rest I mixed and matched to blend, contrast or accent.

Planning an outfit was simple: pick a basic tone and add another color or two for contrast. Fashion trends told you which colors went together, such as or orange and yellow in the sixties or navy blue and lime green, a la Jackie Kennedy.

Normal people wore brown and beige or black and gray. Or if you were really daring, maybe burgundy with pink. Anything else left you open to citation by the fashion police.

Which reminds me. In 1970 I had a color-blind driver's education teacher who should have been arrested for wearing too many shades of green.

This guy mixed his greens like a mad scientist in a chemistry lab. Yellow-green, blue-green, olive green, kelly—in stripes, plaids and solids—you name it, he wore it, all in one outfit.

In the '80s I worked as a color consultant. You remember—one of those trained experts who shined a 1500-watt light in your face, examined your skin tone, hair roots and eye color, and draped you in your best hues. I could detect which shades made you look sensational and which made you look worse than last week's meatloaf.

It was all about the seasons. Are you a late winter, or an early spring with a splash of fall?

I used to ponder: If a winter woman marries an autumn man, can they have a spring baby? Or was that a May-December marriage with a hint of summer?

Using *Color Me Beautiful* as my bible, I never went clothes shopping without my trusty fabric swatches. It made decisions a snap and it worked beautifully for dressing the children, too.

I should have known my kids would react against such a strict upbringing. My Favorite Dotter hates purple. And when Son One hit the teenage years, he deliberately wore a bright orange shirt—definitely not his color—just to irk me. His idea of rebellion, I guess.

But now I'm the one having a midlife color crisis.

Startling numbers of young people are changing the rules. They're wearing beige with gray, navy with black, green with brown. My fashion foundations are shaken and I don't know where to turn.

When in doubt, I turn to the kitchen.

Not to the refrigerator, but to the kitchen sink, where the only item truly unfazed by color trends still resides: the sponge.

"Who chooses sponge colors, anyway?" I asked my husband, "and why do they glow in the dark?"

"So they won't get lost," he said helpfully.

Sponges come in blinding yellow, garish green, neon blue and perky pink. Unchanged by time, these rubberized rectangles have never blended with any kitchen décor known to humankind.

But they still proliferate on store shelves like bunnies in the bushes.

In a world that's changing by the second, it's comforting to know there are still some colors we can count on.

Last week during the Fourth of July, I appreciated another color combination that has stood the test of time—red, white and blue. ▼

BIRTH ORDER BLUES

IT STINKS TO be the middle child.

Just ask Son Two who is now 21 and turned out well considering his unfortunate placement in our family's birth order.

From what I've heard, some middle children have it rough. They can get lost in the shuffle, stuck in the middle, caught between brothers and sisters whom they alternately admire and despise.

In the spirit of Erma Bombeck who wrote each of her three children a letter telling them "I always loved you best," I thought it fitting to shine the spotlight on our middle child for a moment. He agreed this might be fair since his sister's letters to the tooth fairy were featured a few weeks ago.

When I went to look for Son Two's writings, the cupboard was bare. In my faded folder of cards and notes, his offerings were few and far between.

I guess he did more writing on his body than on paper. My favorite was the tattoo he drew on his stomach, all caps, that looked like WOW to him and MOM to me.

He's always been more a person of action than words. As a toddler he spoke little, making his points mainly through body language. Nowadays we just burp our ABC's to communicate.

Only three samples of his early writing still exist.

The first is a valentine from age nine. "To Mom: Thank you for being nice to me. Thank you for letting me beat up my brother when I want."

The next specimen was found neatly taped to his older brother's pillow: "If I find out that you have ever used my stereo I'm going to kick your a**. Your loving bro." –7th grade

Fast-forward to the late teenage years for this gem, probably penned in response to a to-do list I had posted for him.

"Mom—here is a checklist of things YOU must do:

1. Clean yourself up. You're a mess.
2. Make me a sandwich.
3. Take your vitamins with a tall glass of shut up juice. Before you go to bed tonight, Saturday."

Every family needs at least one kid who makes them laugh, and Son Two is ours. Resourceful and resilient, his people skills are legendary. He majored in Schmooziology in college and today can schmooze in three different languages.

He's the flexible one who, at age 3, comforted his older brother crying over the green eggs and ham I served for April Fool's Day breakfast.

"It's okay, they taste just as good. Can I have yours?"

Of course it's possible his taste buds were still damaged from the freshly varnished pretzel wreaths he had eaten the previous Christmas during craft making time.

He's the budding entrepreneur who set up a lemonade stand out front and got his little sister to do all the work.

He's the adventurous one who planned a skydiving trip and talked the other two into going with him.

He's the sweet one who always has a hug ready.

Tucked into the back of my keepsake folder, I found a little gift from the ghost of childhood past.

"Free!! You just won a Mother's Day Coupon Book." It contains one car wash, one game of tennis, and one dishwashing, all of which expired the following month.

But wait—here are a few I forgot about—a free breakfast in bed, a free lunch and a free dinner. Expiration date: Never.

I think it's time to call in some coupons. ▼

GENDER GAB

IT HAPPENS AROUND America a million times a day. Strangers meet, shake hands, and within 10 seconds they're chatting away like old friends.

I'm talking about men, of course—on the subject of sports.

Have you ever observed this phenomenon for yourself?

Take any person of the male persuasion, stick him in a social setting with another macho man, and let the games begin.

The sports connection transcends all ages, races, religions, occupations, socio-economic levels and political viewpoints.

I was attending a University of Southern California football game with my husband when I first noticed it. Son One met us afterward with a crowd of his friends and their parents. Introductions were made all around, and instantly the men were off and running with their favorite topic.

Meanwhile, the women smiled politely and tiptoed over conversational terrain, trying to avoid potential land mines.

"So, how are your kids?" You tried for 20 years and couldn't have any.

"And your son?" Too bad he flunked out last semester.

"What do you do?" By the time we determined whether she worked inside the home, outside the home or volunteered, I was sorry I asked.

Yes, women's conversational ground is fraught with pitfalls. And last night it happened again.

There we sat, riding in a car on our way to a baseball game with two other couples, one of whom we see about once a year, and the other, good friends of theirs who we'd met once before briefly.

I pulled out my stash of chocolate and handed it around to the ladies as an ice breaker. Now there's a universal language—chocolate. We nibbled for a minute and then it was gone. Fingernails drummed on the armrest.

The men galloped away on their standard subject with the reckless abandon of kids getting out of school for the summer. This topic lasted for three hours in the car and two hours at the game.

Meanwhile, the three women hunted for a common theme.

Books? Two of us liked to read, but the other didn't.

Kids? Again, two out of three had kids.

Men? We couldn't talk about them because they were in the car, too.

From shopping and makeup to jewelry and clothes, we went two-for-three every time.

Women who talk about sports are looked upon with suspicion by both genders.

Case in point was the female sportscaster who interviewed the game-winning pitcher on TV. The men were busy admiring the woman's physical attributes, and the women wondered how the gal ever got the job.

The only subject we gals could all relate to was hormones. When we hit upon this topic, it was better than a grand slam in the bottom of the ninth.

PMS, hot flashes, menopause—now that's an animated conversation you'd love to overhear. As the poor souls who sat around us at the game could attest, it was a verbal Energizer Bunny. It kept going and going and going.

There isn't a guy alive who'd be caught dead talking about estrogen or progesterone cream, but by the end of the evening, we had one husband offering to rub the stuff all over his wife. They even stopped at my house to pick up a personal supply.

I'm still looking for the ultimate female topic that will interest women of all ages. Until it comes along, I think it's safest to stick with chocolate.

You'll never catch me asking, "How about those Padres?" ▼

TRASH INTO TREASURES

IT'S TOO HOT to walk.

Believe me, I tried this morning and just couldn't pull it off.

It's the weekend, so of course I slept in and missed the crack-of-dawn, early-rising crowd of dedicated walkers out to beat the heat. How bad can it be, I thought at midmorning, donning my coolest walking shorts, tank top, visor and sunglasses.

And don't forget the 45 SPF lip balm, even though I know I'll regret the awful taste before I'm finished.

My husband was on his way to the gym. Ah, think of exercising in the comfort of air conditioning; I considered the option but decided on no smelly, recycled air for me. I like to walk in the great outdoors.

When I got to the top of the hill, a distance of at least half a block, the siren song of a garage sale called out to me. I trotted over to check it out. A mere seven dollars would buy me enough stocking stuffers to outfit the whole clan next Christmas, so I backtracked home to get some cash.

I'll pick up my goodies at the end of the walk so I won't have to carry them the whole way, I decided.

Back up the street I hiked and turned the other direction, only to be greeted by another sale, which—for the record—I did pass up.

By the next corner I was convinced it was truly too warm to be out walking, so cutting my route short, I headed toward home, only to see two more garage sales lurking in the next block.

This might not sound dangerous to you, but I happen to be a recovering garage sale addict. You can't tell it at first glance, but for a good five years of my life, every Saturday morning I greeted the world with the words, "Let's go sailing—*garage* sailing!"

My children would yelp and run for cover as I fired up the minivan and set out to troll the neighborhoods.

"One man's trash is another man's treasure," I quoted when my husband questioned my purchases. "One girl's discard is another girl's dream."

In an earlier era I drove around on the night before trash pickup to scavenge larger items. One time I balanced a wooden picnic table atop the car and inched my way home, a triumphant hunter-gatherer. It looked great to me.

"That's a piece of trash," said Mr. Right.

"But we need a table on our patio," I argued.

The next evening I smugly served dinner outside and sat down to eat at our new-to-you dining surface. As soon as the kids put their elbows down at one end, a loose board swung upward and whacked us at the other end. I don't remember if my husband ever said, "I told you so," but I know he gave me The Look.

So you can see why a trip down the sale-laced sidewalk was a bit of a test for me this morning. It took no effort at all to slide right back into my old habits. With a limited amount of cash and no appetite for a walk, I swerved into both driveways and ended up with a new backgammon game and a lovely purple necklace.

Aw, why not? I doubled back and hit the house I'd passed up before, then hoofed it to the original scene of the crime. With only five dollars left in my pocket, it gave me pretty good haggling power, and I walked away with as much as I could carry.

When a bargain beckons, who am I to resist?

Maybe I'll try walking again tonight when it cools off and the sun goes down.

By then, all I'll have to fight off is the mosquitoes. ▼

WEIGHING IN

"HATE YOUR FAT? Move it," the ad shouted to me from Thursday's newspaper.

"Just what I need!" I thought. Call the moving van. And make it a big one.

Then I read the fine print: "Fat transfer is an effective means of rebuilding areas of the face. The abdomen and lateral thigh areas provide the best fat for this procedure." No kidding.

"Fat can be frozen and stored for later touchups." Oh good, I'll clear out some freezer space right now.

My personal fight against fat, battle of the bulge, chipping away at chub—whatever your euphemism of choice—has spanned more than four decades.

I've signed on the back of my driver's license to become a fat donor, but they've never taken me up on the offer.

A few years back I joined a program where you become a lifetime member once you reach your goal, after which you only have to weigh in once a month. There's no charge as long as you stay within two pounds of your magic number.

You could say my goal of not paying has become more important to me than my weight goal. And I've learned some tricks along the way that I can share with you. They don't call us Lifers for nothing.

First of all, it's crucial to set the right target weight. If you aim too low, you just end up raising it later. And you only get to increase it once, so my theory is: Aim high. An inflated figure will pay off in the long run.

Next, be sure to select the proper wardrobe for that monthly weigh-in. Did you know you can use the handy little food scale for weighing your clothes? Choose those that will let you slide in under the wire.

Forget about those low-cal foods and point-counting bracelets—they ought to sell featherweight underwear. You might find yourself shivering in bare feet, nylon shorts and a tank top in December, but it's all about the sacrifices.

Finally, never underestimate the power of mind games. Some of my favorites are: I Don't Really Have to Watch My Weight, Denial Is Tasty, and How Long Can I Wait This Month before Cutting Back.

Like the telltale drop in the pit of the stomach when your plane starts its descent for landing, you can feel the moment when it's time to get prepare for the monthly day of reckoning.

Believe me, I've had some close calls. There have been times when I waited too long to start my final approach for the weigh-in. And it wasn't pretty.

One time at weigh-in after I had already taken off every clothing item possible without breaking public decency laws, the Weight Warden kindly said, "The scale is blinking, you're right on the borderline. Would you like to remove your watch and glasses?"

"Sure, if you think that'll help," I said. It didn't. I knew I should have bought heavier glasses.

"You're so close," she persisted. "Is there anything else you can remove?"

I got ready to strip off my tank top right then and there until I saw the horrified expression of a man third back in line. He looked blurry because my glasses were off.

She finally gave me the benefit of the doubt, and I escaped once again to go out and load up on all the things I'd given up for the past week.

A smarter person would have worn a catheter for the preceding 24 hours. An even smarter person would just lose the five pounds and be done with it, but where's the fun in that?

It's time to call the fat movers to see if they make house calls. ▼

AGING IS IN THE EYE OF THE BEHOLDER

I CAUGHT SON Two staring down at my forehead the other day. He can't really help it, since he towers over me at 6 feet 2 inches, but I demanded to know what he was looking at.

"Nothing."

But I knew better. He was checking out those grooves on my brow, furrows so deep you could drive a John Deer tractor through them.

I'm a little jealous of Sally Field, described in a recent interview as having a forehead "laddered with expression lines." Just like me, I thought—laddered. I've got a real stairway to heaven on my face.

When I mentioned the phrase to Mr. Right, he offered his own opinion.

"That's because Sally Field has one of the largest foreheads in America, second only to Helen Hunt," he said.

I'd never thought about it that way before. I guess on the big screen, you have to expect that everything is, well, bigger. And they probably use industrial strength Spackle to fill in the lines for the camera.

No matter how you measure, it all boils down to aging, which I've come to believe—like beauty—is in the eye of the beholder.

This golden nugget of truth was thrust upon me last fall when my husband and I traveled to Tennessee to visit our former college on its 50th anniversary. I thought it was a perfect way to stretch out my 50th birthday.

We found ourselves in the lobby of our alma mater, chatting with people we hadn't seen for 25 to 30 years. Spying one couple who were friends from the 1980s, we eagerly rushed over to say hello and were a bit surprised when we had to introduce ourselves.

The couple honestly didn't recognize us. I tell myself it's because we were out of context, and maybe they didn't expect to see us there. This couple looked almost the same as before, give or take a few decades and 20 or 30 pounds. Surely they hadn't forgotten us.

I'll never forget the woman's parting words, and I quote them exactly.

"I'm just wondering," she asked, "do we look as old to you as you look to us?"

My hearing must be going, I thought. Did she really say that out loud?

Her words made me feel worse than a pimple on prom night. I was so nonplussed that for once I fell silent. Only afterward did an assortment of snappy comebacks spring to mind.

Perhaps she was getting back at me for asking if her two-year-old son was her grandchild. After all, how many 48-year-old women do you know who are still bearing children? This gal was the Mick Jagger of motherhood. So it's possible my faux pas could have rattled her.

Later that weekend we ran into our former sociology professor, who, amazingly, still remembered both our names and the position my husband had played on the college baseball team.

He exclaimed that we didn't look any older. I gave him a big hug and complimented him on his eyesight.

It proves that aging truly *is* in the eye of the beholder. ▼

WEDDING WOES

A ROMANTIC CRUISE to an exotic island with the man of my dreams? Or maybe it was the express boat to Catalina for a few days. Whatever you want to call it, Mr. Right and I celebrated our 30th wedding anniversary last week.

Fortunately, we got married in an era when throwing a wedding didn't cost as much as feeding an entire Third World country.

In those days the biggest choice we had to make was what brand of nuts and mints to serve. My only departure from a traditional cake-and-punch menu was to buy ice cream bonbons, which ended up melting in the church kitchen.

It used to be that you went on a destination honeymoon. Nowadays the whole wedding is a destination. The way I see it, the destination-wedding concept has it all backwards. You're supposed to take a trip to get away from all the people at home, not bring them along with you. If you're going to fly the entire wedding party to Hawaii, the honeymooners might as well spend the week in Barstow.

But there are still ways to cut costs.

For only $29.95, just about anyone can perform a wedding ceremony. You don't have to hire a pastor—simply pay for a family member or friend to act as your own clergy-for-a-day.

However, if you choose to go the budget route, you should beware of a few pitfalls, some finer points not mentioned in the basic starter package.

Contrary to public opinion, the most important words spoken at a wedding are not, "I now pronounce you husband and wife." They are three little words that most guests take for granted: "Please be seated."

At several nuptials we attended this year, the amateur up front never got the memo about when to utter these words. So we, the people, remained standing, shifting from foot to foot, wondering when we could decently sink into our chairs.

Okay, I confess. I might have been the one to start the seating movement.

Call it the wave—in reverse. Row by row, starting from the back, we gradually sat down until only the mother of the bride was left standing. Someone finally tapped her on the shoulder.

Then there's the issue of being able to hear. Trained orators know how to project their voices. Chances are, they have a degree in Speaking Loudly. But do-it-yourselfers often need some help.

At one recent wedding we attended, the DJ had a microphone, but the person officiating did not. Go figure.

The guests had to pretend we could hear. And the only audible phrase that drifted back to us was a real stumper. The couple apparently wrote their own vows, one of which was, "I promise to keep my sense of humor."

Keep your sense of humor? Everyone knows that's the first thing you lose after your savings account and your slim figure. What were they thinking?

That's like saying, "I promise not to snore." Nobody can guarantee such a thing, and they shouldn't even try.

I respect people's efforts to economize, but you have to draw the line somewhere. If you ask me, they should leave wedding officiating to the professionals.

Our daughter has a great money-saving wedding plan. She says when it's her turn, she'll order a giant submarine sandwich and a few bags of chips and call it a reception. At least that's what she said when she was 12, and by golly, we're holding her to it. ▼

PART TWO

Fall

.

AT ZIT'S END

I HAD A big one last night, a real beauty of an eruption, right in the crease of my cheek.

In the morning it wasn't big enough to catch, so I let it go (to use a fishing metaphor). For most of the day I pretended it was invisible, tried to hide it by smiling so it would sink into the wrinkle that runs from my nose to the corner of my mouth.

In the afternoon it grew. At a party I attended late in the day, people's eyes were drawn toward it as if to a magnet, a huge train wreck of a blemish. They couldn't help themselves.

By nightfall, it was undeniably ripe, but the stubborn spot wouldn't surrender without a fight.

After performing outpatient surgery, I looked around for a remedy to dab on top. I knew I'd seen a list of offbeat cures on the internet, but couldn't recall the antidote for acne.

Was it Colgate toothpaste or Listerine mouthwash? Horseradish and vinegar or Hunt's tomato paste?

If you've seen the movie, *My Big Fat Greek Wedding*, you'll know why I almost reached for the Windex bottle.

First thing the next morning I went online and located the missing list of household hints.

"Cover the blemish with a dot of honey and place a Band-Aid over it. Honey kills the bacteria, keeps the skin sterile and speeds healing. Works overnight," it stated.

I haven't checked this out on TruthorFiction.com, but I figure it's worth a try. And fortunately there's a honey bear standing at attention in the pantry.

While I'm at it, there are a few more remedies on the list I might try. It prescribes Altoids for a stuffy nose, horseradish and olive oil for muscle aches, Alka-Seltzer for bladder infections, Heinz vinegar for bruises, Quaker Oats for arthritis pain, and Elmer's glue for splinter removal—a whole wellness clinic right here in my own cupboard.

It's ironic that a woman my age still needs to struggle with a teenage skin problem. You'd think by this time I'd have outgrown it. Obviously it's another one of life's little injustices.

I'm not alone in my pain. Last week I got together with my longtime friend Debbie from junior high.

She loves to remind me at least once per decade that I was the laughingstock of the class because my mom wouldn't let me wear a bra as early as the rest of the girls. Undershirts in seventh grade weren't cool—although they did save me from the strap-snapping antics popular with boys of that era.

And let's not talk about the delayed leg-shaving issues I endured during those years. Picture fishnet stockings with tufts of hair sticking out and you get the gist.

But back to my visit with Debbie. She made a statement that's stayed with me.

"It's not fair that we have wrinkles and zits at the same time."

I couldn't have put it better myself. At this age we should have attained some measure of immunity, some no-fault blemish insurance, like a good-driver discount, to balance out the other stresses of life.

Why must we have middle-school angst along with our midlife crises? It's just wrong.

If you can't relate to this, you are either one of the lucky women who is sailing through life un-pimpled, or you're a man.

Either way, you've got it made. ▼

THE FAINTING GENE

IS FAINTING HEREDITARY?

I'm asking because we have both fainters and nonfainters in our family, a fifty/fifty split between my husband and me, with our kids landing on both sides of the great divide.

Right from the start I knew that my husband was a fainter. He never tried to hide it from me or sneak it into any prenuptial statement such as, "This marriage will be null and void if the groom passes out during the wedding."

Weddings don't faze him. It's hospitals that give him a problem, which it turns out is an occupational hazard.

During his years as pastor of a local church, he warned his congregation that they'd have to be in serious condition before he'd visit them in the hospital.

"You don't ever want to be that sick," he said.

His usual hospital strategy was to send me ahead to chat with the patient for a while. Then he'd pop in and offer a quick prayer before retreating to the hallway to put his head between his knees.

In all other crisis situations, Mr. Right is a rock of calm, cool collectedness.

Take, for instance, the day when our young daughter stuck a Tic Tac up her nose. (We later found out this was on a dare from Son Two.) She felt smug for a while until the candy coating melted off. Then the burn set in and she started howling. Panicked, I shined a flashlight into the nostril and tried to dig it out with tweezers.

My husband walked onto the scene, calmly assessed the situation, and with one swift motion, gave a downward squeeze on the bridge of her nose. Out popped the offending candy, sanity was restored and her nose smelled minty fresh for the rest of the day.

So you can see that he's much more cool-headed than I am in the face of disaster. Unless it involves a trip to the hospital. Then we're in trouble.

To be fair, he was helpful enough getting me to the ER the day I broke my wrist falling down in the driveway. But when it came time for them to set the fracture, he suddenly had urgent business at Burger King.

"It's not about the blood or the needles," he explains. "It's the general smell of the hospital. Something about it makes me light-headed."

Case in point was the time Favorite Dotter had her adenoids removed. Things went well during the surgery and they wheeled her into the recovery area. Only one parent could sit with the patient at a time, so I took my turn first.

After a while I traded shifts with my husband and left for a bathroom break. I was gone no longer than a minute when I heard myself being paged over the loudspeaker.

"Mrs. Swagerty, please return to the recovery room. Mrs. Swagerty, return immediately to recovery."

Fearing disaster, picturing our poor daughter hemorrhaging or worse, I rushed back—only to find Mr. Right on a couch with nurses hovering, an oxygen mask clamped to his face. That was the last time I left him in charge at the hospital.

I'm afraid he's passed the fainting gene down to Son One, who once got up from the dentist's chair and collapsed on the floor. Fortunately the dentist had oxygen on hand, but I suspect there've been other unreported incidents.

Which brings me back to my original question. Is it possible that fainting, along with snoring and cowlicks, is an inherited trait? This could be the next great genetic discovery.

If so, I want the credit. ▼

INTERVIEWING FOR DUMMIES

LAST WEEK I went on my first job interview in 25 years.

In retrospect I realize that I should have worn a big badge that said, "Hello, My Name Is Clueless," but I'm sure it was obvious.

When I first got the phone call to come in for the interview, a smarter person would have run right out and bought a copy of "Interviewing for Dummies." But not me. I thought, I can handle this.

The ordeal opened with an office skills test consisting of four tasks: make an Excel spreadsheet of names and addresses, write a letter, merge the addresses with the letter, and tell how you would merge the mailing labels—all in 30 minutes.

A mail merge—are they kidding? Even people who do it all the time can't remember how to do a mail merge.

The admin locked me in a small room with a timer and a computer. On your mark, get set, go. I felt like a fairytale character, imprisoned in an attic and given an impossible task: Spin this straw into gold.

As soon as she left, I whipped out my cell phone and called my husband.

"Hi Honey, can you tell me how to do a mail merge?" I asked.

I figured even game show contestants get to phone a friend. And if that didn't work, I still had time to poll the audience.

It took me 10 minutes to find the Excel template. From there it was a frenzy of typing, and me without my special computer glasses. I had also left my elbow supports and carpal tunnel wrist guard at home. First impressions are important, you know.

Time was up and we moved on to the next gauntlet, the Committee of Six. The human resources person gave me a sheet of questions to look at before I went to sit in the hot seat. Little did I know they would go right down the page, line by line, word for word and ask each one.

"What attracted you to the job?" they asked as the opening query. On and on I blathered about the hours, the schedule, the health benefits, what a great place it was to work, what's in it for me—yadda yadda.

Later, the light dawned: they probably just wanted to know which items on the job description I could perform.

There's a mental forehead smack for you.

Sailing through the next few questions, I hit my stride: "Tell about a time you handled a challenge successfully," they asked.

A story from my teaching days about handling a vomiting kid went over great. When in doubt, make 'em laugh.

But the next item wiped the smile off my face.

"Tell about a situation when you met a challenge unsuccessfully and what you learned from it."

Suddenly, my palms were slippery and my bladder felt as tight as a fat lady wearing spandex.

How could I narrow it down to only one failure? I hemmed and hawed and came up with a whole lot of nothing.

Afterwards, when I got home and reported to my 19-year-old daughter, she couldn't believe how inept I'd been.

"Mom, if they give you the questions ahead of time, you ought to have an answer ready," she said.

She's the job-hunting pro. I should have consulted her.

If I learned one thing from this experience, it's that interviewing isn't for sissies.

And if I ever get another chance, I'll be sure to prepare. I'll have that name badge ready and my cell phone charged. ▼

A BAD HAIR LIFE

I'VE WORN THE same boring hairstyle for 40 years.

Maybe not continuously, but my current hairdo looks suspiciously similar to my fifth-grade school picture. Take away the stretchy headband and the goofy teeth and you've got a match.

To be truthful, it looks a lot better on me now than it did then. What was my mother thinking, saddling an 11-year-old with a middle-aged hairstyle? I shouldn't blame her, she was only doing her best, and after all, everyone looked bad in the '60s.

Maybe that's why I went a little crazy in the '70s and ended up with a curly perm that resembled a dandelion ready to blow.

Afros were all the rage, even my husband tried it out for a few years. Our own personal hair-trainer, Emilio, came over to our house and gave perms in the kitchen sink. I think we got a group rate when our two best friends jumped on the bandwagon too.

What can I say? It was the '70s and we were looking for curls in all the wrong places.

In the '80s I tried out the layered look, which my kids call a mullet. They roll on the floor and shriek, "Mullet alert, mullet alert" while watching home videos from that era. Which just proves my point: you can't win.

I should have been a man. Nobody blames males for keeping their hairstyle unchanged for decades on end. There's not all that unhealthy pressure to keep up with the times.

Not that I don't admire people who change their hairstyle. It's just that I've never been able to pull it off. In the past five years I've managed to grow out my bangs, and that's about it for variety. This summer I pulled my hair back in a rubber band, but there's nothing flattering about a one-inch ponytail.

Then there's the issue of paying attention to hair. I think there are two kinds of people: those who notice hairdo changes and those who don't. And they're usually married to each other.

Sad to say, I'm the unobservant one in my household and it drives the observant ones crazy. It frustrates my daughter no end when I fail to admire her latest cut or dye job. So much so that I've resorted to throwing out random compliments just in case, such as, "I like what you've done with your hair." (This also works well in the office setting.)

But even the best intentions can backfire if you're too earnest about it. The other night my husband went out to get a haircut, and upon his return I was careful to comment.

"Nice haircut," I said.

He looked at me quizzically. "I didn't get one," he said. "The haircut store was closed."

You can't fault a girl for trying.

I've never been very good at communicating with hairdressers, either. My vocabulary just doesn't jibe with theirs. A simple request such as "Don't take any off the sides" translates into "Go ahead and shear me bald" in stylist-speak.

Once you find a hair artist who makes you look like a million bucks, you should hold them close and never let them go. Not on vacation, not to Europe, and definitely not into retirement. You should keep them on retainer for the rest of their life.

So that's why, since I've finally found a decent style, I plan to stick with it.

When the day comes for my kids to choose a picture for the undertaker, they can pick a photo from now.

I'm sure I'll still be wearing the same hairdo then. ▼

CAKED CUL-DE-SAC CAUSES CONJECTURE

IT WAS A picture of carnage: little heaps of red, white and brown matter splattered in the street with tire marks tracing designs over the top.

There were eerie smears of colored icing and chocolate cake already setting into rigor mortis, not yet fully hardened. I came upon the crusty crime scene on my morning walk and it set my mind to wondering.

What happened here?

Empty calories were strewn willy-nilly in the street. Cupcake carcasses were left to spoil in the sun. Crummy fragments formed a perfect circle within the cul-de-sac. And why were there no ants?

It's not as if it were the morning after Halloween, when you expect to find a few smashed pumpkins in the road. It was an ordinary weekday morning in September, teeming with unanswered questions.

I felt like an archeologist stumbling upon Stonehenge, seeing the remains embedded in the pavement and pondering what ancient rituals could have caused such a pattern.

Was it the leftover debris from a birthday party run amok? Or a forgetful parent who set a batch of cupcakes on the car roof and drove away unaware. Could there have been a collision of bakery truck and trash truck? But there were no car parts, only cake parts.

There's probably a simple solution to the mystery, I thought.

It could have been a party game, an outdoor version of Pin the Tail on the Donkey played with pastries and a moving target.

Or perhaps it was a creative session of batting practice for tomorrow's T-ball game. Maybe the coach balanced a cupcake on the tee and said, "Let's see how far this baby will fly."

Possibly there was a frustrated dieter cleaning out the cupboards, punctuating the words with overhand hurls. "Get. These. Outta. Here."

Maybe it was a food fight—every kid's fantasy and every mother's nightmare. Imagine the blacktop battlefield littered with crumb bombs lobbed through the air and kids yelling.

But to be honest, how many people do you know who've actually been in a food fight? I've never experienced one myself, unless you count those college fraternity flicks or the Lost Boys on a rampage in the movie *Hook*.

It's a lot like amnesia. Do you know anyone who's ever had it? I bet you could travel six degrees of separation and still not find a person with amnesia. It's as rare as a brush fire in the rainforest, yet it's a staple of TV shows, movies and book plots.

Getting back to food fights, I'll be the first to admit that I've led a sheltered life. My parents set strict table rules: No food flinging, even in emergencies. The closest we ever came was when a rogue can of whipped cream squirted across the room on Thanksgiving Day. And you can bet the squirter was severely scolded.

I've heard that a real food fight is a highly overrated experience. A few years ago, a movie crew came to Magnolia Elementary in Carlsbad and rented out the school cafeteria to film a food battle. Afterwards, the staff said the fake mashed potatoes were disappointing, the retakes were tedious and cleaning up the Jell-o stains took all summer.

There's a thought—maybe the street was used for a movie set.

We may never know what happened in that quiet, suburban neighborhood, and I'm not asking for an explanation.

But if it was a food fight, next time I want an invitation. ▼

VACUUMING THE ROOF

IF CLEANLINESS IS next to godliness, our neighbors up the street are on the fast track to heaven.

This morning there was a man vacuuming their roof. He wasn't just giving it a light once over, or a lick and a promise, as my mother used to say. He was getting down between the cracks with a little round brush attachment.

I've never been known for my housekeeping skills, but cleaning the roof isn't on my list of long-term goals. It's not even on my list of things to put off indefinitely, like filling in my children's baby books or scheduling a gum graft.

In the first place, how did the guy get the vacuum up there? I can barely hoist mine down from the heater closet to the floor without using a forklift.

Secondly, where in the Yellow Pages would you look to find the right person for the job? I don't think Merry Maids would like it if you asked them to do your roof. It's hard enough to find someone who does windows, let alone shingles.

Call me naive, but I've never heard of roof cleaners, and I carry some pretty impressive credentials.

At the end of my senior year of high school, I won the coveted Betty Crocker Homemaker of the Year award. This was back when home economics and wood shop were part of the curriculum. Dinosaurs also roamed the earth.

The unexpected honor was a triumph that left most of my family and friends shaking their heads in disbelief. All except for young Mr. Right, who filed it away for future reference when selecting a wife.

The contest had nothing to do with scrubbing or sanitation, but I remember one question about hard-boiling eggs. It was probably more about knowing how to take a multiple-choice test than knowing how to cook. Some people called me Betty Crocker from then on. I don't think it was a compliment.

Over the years guests have exclaimed at how clean our home is, but it's just an illusion. Tidy, maybe, but never clean. Doing away with clutter is my main strategy. I believe if you leave the dust undisturbed, no one will notice it.

When our daughter was young, we gathered the dust bunnies, gave them names and called them pets. This was an improvement from her roly-poly collection in the backyard.

Once I worked with a gal who was the queen of clean. She came from a long line of Dutch neatniks and her house showed it. On my first visit to her house, I admired her spotless shower door tracks and asked her how she did it.

"I use a toothbrush," she confided.

"I brush daily, too" I said, "but how do you keep your door tracks so clean?"

My jaw dropped in horror as the light dawned. And here I'd been throwing away my old toothbrushes. Never again. Now I save them religiously. In fact, I have a whole collection.

Our neighbor across the street is the Donald Trump of house hygiene. He polishes the windows for his wife and even scours the driveway. His grass sprouts with neatly aerated lawn turds on a regular schedule. We gave up trying to compete years ago.

It looks to me as if the newly vacuumed roof up the street has upped the ante.

As for us, my husband the do-it-yourselfer is talking about replacing our 19-year-old roof with a new one next year.

The way I see it now, we don't need a new roof—we just need to vacuum the one we have. ▼

EVERYBODY LOVES A MYSTERY

CHALK IT UP to watching too many episodes of "CSI" or reading Nancy Drew and Hardy Boys books as kids. Readers responded as never before to my column, "Caked Cul-de-sac Causes Conjecture," and here are some of their comments.

"You mean to tell me that you and Mr. Right have never had a food fight? Oh my gosh, Bill and I have food fights all the time. More frequently before the new kitchen. However, we have pictures of me with guacamole all over my head and some Lipton soup with those little noodles on top. You have not lived until you have had a food fight. Of course our kids think we are nuts." —Twila

"NO FOOD FIGHTS? You just don't impress me as the type to lead such a sheltered life. I say the next time that son of yours is home you just let it rip. The best way is to come up behind him with a nice motherly hug, telling him how much you miss him and then gently smear the chocolate pudding around his ears and cheeks and the back of his neck.

We have very strict rules for food fights at our home: All flinging is to take place out side the house. Smearing is permitted in the kitchen. No rinsing your sister off with the power washer AFTER the food fight.

And if you are naked while participating in a food fight, by all means stay INSIDE the house."—Shari

"Solve the mystery? I can barely pronounce the title. But you sure had a lot of creative suggestions. What a waste of dessert." — Karen

"I'm voting for the 'forgot the tray of cupcakes on the roof of the car' scenario. What a waste of good chocolate." —Alice

Tina contributed another UFO (Unexplained Food Outside) sighting.

"This past week, I saw a cheesecake with strawberries on top near the gutter, obviously complete when it hit the pavement. I've wondered all week what happened. My guess is that a couple had a fight on their way to celebrate something, and somebody flung the thing out the window to prove a point."

"I think the cheesecake in the gutter and the cake in the cul-de-sac are somehow linked," said Steve. "It's a conspiracy."

And then there's the reader, Nan, who called in the spelling police. "Did you mean crummy or crumby?"

Okay, so I lied. At the end of the column I said I didn't need an explanation, but the truth is, inquiring minds want to know.

Here's the real scoop sent in by a reader named Ruth:

"Picture two giddy gals, celebrating the last night home before one heads off to college, mom safely tucked away in slumber.

"Picture a huge 'bon voyage' cake from Costco on the kitchen counter, calling their names. Midnight darkness hides the bathing-suit–clad sisters' fling.

"Picture a predawn departure, car laden with worldly goods, Mom pulls out of the driveway and headlights pierce the scene.

"What happened here?! And off they go.

"Much later, mom returns home and is greeted by flocks of crows enjoying the gala buffet. Mom gathers all the hoses, like a fireman to the rescue and braves the dive-bombing feathered friends.

"The party now just a memory, mom enters the empty house and follows the tiny crumbs of chocolate up the stairs, sits on the daughter's bed and smiles. Yes, summer break has been good and all will be well.

"She catches herself thinking, sure hope I can control myself next time I see cake." ▼

PARALLEL PARKING

PARALLEL PARKING IS one of life's simple pleasures—and it's calorie free.

Not to brag, but this is one area in which I pride myself. If parallel parking were an Olympic event, I'd be a gold medalist.

And I don't even need to drive my own car. To borrow a verse from Dr. Seuss's *Green Eggs and Ham,* I can do it in a van, I can do it in a truck. I can do it in a sports car or an SUV. Just call me the Sam-I-Am of parking.

The most satisfying way to pull it off is a clean sweep on the first try. One smooth slide with no adjustments needed, no messy jockeying back and forth.

If I need to pull out and start over, that's okay, too. I still count it as a win, as long as nobody was watching.

I'm not known for my spatial skills, per se. I can't judge distances or figure out how to fold down the flaps of a cardboard box in the right order. But when it comes to parallel parking, even my own kids are amazed at my prowess.

"How'd you do that, Mom?" they ask, hopping out of the car to find my tires perfectly aligned with the curb.

Some people circle around for blocks, searching for a place to nose in on an angle rather than attempting the dreaded parking maneuver. Not me—I relish it.

I drive around looking for a just enough curb space to make it challenging. Angled parking doesn't even count in my book. That's for beginners, not worthy of my expertise.

All the credit goes back to my high school driving instructor who made us memorize his 12-step program for perfect parking. His words echo in my ears every time I pull up alongside the curb and flip on my blinker.

This trainer not only had nerves of steel, he also was a genius. By my reckoning, he should be inducted into the driver's training hall of fame, white knuckles and all.

Admittedly, I get a little excited when I execute the perfect parking job. A hissed "Yesssss" and a high five to myself usually takes care of the celebration, or perhaps a little happy dance in the street. Sometimes I check for cameras to see if anyone caught it on film.

Whenever I see other drivers parking with proficiency, I take time to stop and give them two thumbs up, a regular Siskel and Ebert of the curb. Sometimes I get strange looks—not everyone shares my glee.

My husband thinks he's the bomb because he can parallel park on the left side of the street. It's a talent he's perfected since working in downtown San Diego, a maze of a town where every other street goes in the opposite direction.

But I have news for him: I can park on the left-hand side, too. I did it just last week and only nipped the car behind me the teensiest bit, not enough to take off any paint or set off the car alarm.

I believe that the women's movement in this country would gain a little more R-E-S-P-E-C-T if more women mastered the art of parking parallel. There's nothing like it to win the admiration of the men.

So, I'm here to tell you: parking is no longer a male-dominated sport. Say good-bye to the old clichés, "Real men don't eat quiche" and "Real women don't pump gas."

I am woman. Watch me park. ▼

A WORD TO THE WISE

IF YOU CAN'T say something nice, don't say anything at all. Don't count your chickens before they hatch. Never eat yellow snow.

These and other pithy proverbs make up a body of knowledge that I call Words to Live By. Sometimes you come across occasions that cry out for a quote, in which case I'm happy to supply one.

One such moment struck our family the last time we ate at Marie Calendar's restaurant. Favorite Dotter was leaving for her trip to Ireland, and Son Two was on his way to Spain—what better excuse for group overeating?

I tried to order a light meal, soup and salad with cornbread on the side. But when the waiter delivered the food, I almost choked. Industrial sized blocks of yellow cake dwarfed the plates they were carried out on, almost covering the whole table. These babies took up at least a square foot apiece.

"Careful," I warned, "Never eat anything bigger than your head."

I'm a mom—I'm full of maxims.

How were we going to stuff all that food into an organ that's supposedly the size of your fist? I stuck out my own fist and pondered it for a moment, then dove in and did my best. Thank goodness for take-home boxes. It looked like Christmas later on our kitchen counter.

Each family has its own collection of formulas, and I like to think they rub off on the offspring if they hear them enough times.

Although our daughter phoned home often during her six months away, one time came as a surprise. When I asked why she'd called, she quoted from a wooden sign that used to hang in the kids' bathroom when they were little.

"Rules of Life: Share, obey, be kind, listen, wash, brush, flush, recycle, and *call your mother*," she rattled off.

Money well spent on that plaque, wouldn't you agree?

On the flip side, not following words of wisdom can cause pain. One lesson that I learned the hard way still sticks with me after more than a decade.

The setting was Asilomar Conference Center in Monterey, California. My husband and I attended a conference where I led the singing portion of each session. Feeling inadequate without the band and singers who usually surrounded me, I did my best using only a keyboard for support. It wasn't very comfortable, but I got through it and went on.

Nine months later, out of the blue I received a summary of the evaluation forms that had been handed out at the end of the conference. It was neatly typed. All of the comments were positive, except for one lone statement that had me in tears: "The song leader didn't have a solo-quality voice."

There's always a critic in the crowd, I thought. What kind of person would make a remark like that, let alone write it down? I felt deeply wounded.

A week later I was still smarting from the bad review. When I mentioned it to my husband, he asked, "Didn't you write that yourself?"

The minute he said it, I knew he was right. In a fit of post-conference relief, I had scribbled the comment on the evaluation form just to be funny. I figured they'd recognize my name at the top and throw it out. But I didn't allow for my own forgetfulness.

Since then, I've coined some new words to live by:
Never say anything bad about yourself. The feelings you hurt could be your own. ▼

CARDIAC EVENT

THE BIG ONE happened two Fridays ago while I was shopping at Costco.

Not the great seismic event all Californians dread, but a small, internal earthquake that I've half-expected, half-denied would happen for years.

Living with a family history of heart disease had made me cautious, but decent cholesterol numbers, a healthy diet and regular exercise convinced me I could beat it. Until two weeks ago.

The day before, a Thursday, I was feeling a bit winded during my daily walk. Something was amiss.

I wore my oldest jeans for the rest of the day in case I had to go to the hospital and they'd have to cut my pants off, a horror story I'd heard from a friend.

Then a worse fear hit: what if I had a coronary at the Los Angeles Coliseum where we were headed to a football game that Saturday? We were also slated to meet the parents of Son One's girlfriend for the first time.

Friday morning I wore my new jeans to Costco for my regular shopping trip. I felt tired after pushing my loaded cart to the front of the store. So when I felt faint at the checkout, I sat down and called my husband.

By the time he arrived, there was an elephant stepping on my chest. I lay down on the floor—always an attention getter—and said, "Call 911."

Because we were less than a mile away from the hospital, Mr. Right said, "I can get you there quicker."

On the way he reassured me that I could always get new jeans if needed, which I'm ashamed to say, was my biggest worry. You'd think a person would have profound thoughts at such a moment. Not a chance.

When we arrived at Emergency, they wanted me to go to the waiting room because I hadn't come by ambulance. (Note to self: next time let the professionals handle it.) I pulled out my cell phone and threatened to call 911 from the curb.

"Never mind," they said. We'll take you in.

After a few hours in the ER and getting poked more times than the Pillsbury Doughboy, the doctors determined I'd had a "cardiac event."

That sounds like a party, I thought. Suddenly, I could see the perfect advertising slogan floating in the air above my bed: "Let Costco Cater Your Next Cardiac Event."

"Quick, write that down," I told my husband.

Thanks to the excellent care I received, including an angioplasty and a stent, I went home in fine condition the next day. Good thing, because my husband was nearing his time limit for not fainting in the hospital.

Now, two weeks later, I can see plenty of advantages to living through a heart attack. In fact, I made a list of the top ten reasons it wasn't so bad.

Number 10: You can blame all your memory loss on it.

I forget the other nine.

It's fun to amaze my friends by showing off post-angiogram bruises. I've always been a bruise connoisseur—the bigger and brighter, the better. Now I've got specimens worthy of Cecil B. DeMille, an aurora borealis of colors in lovely autumn hues.

Son Two, the son of few words, even commented, "That's a bruise of epic proportions."

There are still some challenges ahead, such as where to stash that cute little bottle of nitroglycerin when going for a walk without pockets. This morning I tried sticking it in my sports bra, which I'm sure improved my profile.

Then there's the persistent problem of tape residue. After having more than 36 EKG leads attached to my body, I'm stickier than a batch of day-old cotton candy. We're talking world-class stubborn adhesives here.

People tell me I'll soon be back to normal. I say it's not over until the tape residue is gone. ▼

MURPHY'S LAW SCHOOL

WHO IS MURPHY and why does he get blamed for everything that goes wrong?

This is the type of question that strikes at the very heart of our existence on the planet, but you never see anything like it on grad school entrance exams.

Son One took the LSAT (pronounced *el-sat*) last summer for entrance into law school. Have you ever seen the questions on one of those tests? The samples quizzes alone are enough to cure the urge to go to grad school.

One practice question gave the following five answer choices:

a) enthusiastic support, b) bemused dismissal, c) reasoned disagreement, d) strict neutrality, e) guarded agreement.

It's not quite the same as taking a restaurant survey online, where the answers range from Strongly Disagree to Strongly Agree on a scale of 1 to 5. And you can be sure there are no discount coupons when you're finished.

After reading a few sample questions, I began to suspect that the writers took a handful of words, stirred them around, and drew them out of a hat in random combinations. The exam authors had the last laugh, though. My son said the practice test bore little resemblance to the actual exam.

Even more mind-boggling is the array of acronyms for the different tests. There's the LSAT for law, GMAT for business and the MCAT for medical school, to mention a few.

But why limit the tests to only those subjects? I can think of plenty more.

How about the MFAT for weight management, the GVAT for winemakers or the ATBAT for advanced baseball studies? Then there's the IPAT for massage therapists, the XRAT for exterminators, and the ALLWET for scuba divers. Don't forget the LNIÑO for meteorologists. And Dr. Seuss lovers could go for their MCAT in the MHAT.

Imagine all the jobs that could be generated to write these entrance exams. You don't hear me volunteering, because I'm starting my own test, and I'm calling it the LSWAG. Here are some samples questions:

1. How does washing your car guarantee rain the next day?

2. What are the odds that the phone will ring right after you get in the shower when you've been waiting two hours for the call?

3. Why does the item you bought last week go on sale this week?

4. How come you always hit the curb driving home from getting your tires aligned?

5. Why do they invariably open up a new checkout at the grocery store just as you get to the front of the line?

6. Why, when you give away something you haven't used in 10 years, do you find you need it the next day?

7. What causes them to discontinue your brand of hair color as soon as you find one you like?

8. Why does a lost item turn up the day after you buy a replacement?

9. How come a check always arrives in the mail the day after you make your monthly bank deposit?

10. Why does the last wave of trick-or-treaters show up five minutes after you've run out of Halloween candy?

These questions may not tap into the deepest mysteries life, but they certainly are things that make you go "Hmm."

Answer them correctly and I guarantee you admission to Murphy's Law school. I hope my son gets into Murphy's. Now let's talk about student loans. ▼

BY THE HAIR OF MY CHINNY-CHIN-CHIN

"I refuse to think of them as chin hairs. I think of them as stray eyebrows." —*Janette Barber*

WHAT'S THE PROPER etiquette for chin hairs? Did they suddenly become fashionable and someone forgot to send me the memo?

This morning I saw a lady in the post office sporting a chin wart with sassy hairs of various lengths sprouting from it in all directions. These were not wispy strands. They were springy shoots of white hair.

They looked like a tiny bouquet of beheaded flower stems, and I wondered how she got them to stay like that. Standing behind her in a long line gave me the perfect vantage point to gawk. I had to admire this woman's sense of personal style. It was a follicle free-for-all.

It was hard not to stare. The only other female I'd ever seen with such impressive chin growth was a gal in New Hampshire who had one long, curly tendril, the presence of which I chalked up to poor eyesight.

So I ask again, what would Emily Post, the maven of manners, advise? Try not to look? Compliment the person? Reach in your purse and offer your tweezers?

I thought chin hairs were to be avoided at all costs.

While most people plan ahead for advance directives and power of attorney, I made sure to provide for durable power of plucking. It'd be just my luck to have my life saved, only to live in a vegetative state in which I couldn't take care of my own chin grooming.

One of the first things they asked me during my recent hospital stay was if I have an advance directive.

"Yes," I said, "and it includes a chin hair clause."

The nurse looked at me blankly.

It's true. My living will includes a provision for several of my girlfriends to tweeze on my behalf if I ever lapse into a coma. Not something I could entrust to my husband. Sorry, Honey.

Now there's an untapped market niche—a mobile plucking service. It could be named The Sisterhood of the Traveling Tweezers.

The post-office woman's chin hairs wouldn't have lasted long if she were teaching in an elementary school. You can always depend on kids to speak up.

"Mrs. Swagerty, you've got something in your nose," a child informed me one time.

Another day it was, "What's that in your teeth?"

So helpful, those students. Of course they never made a peep the day I wore my shirt inside out. Neither did any of my colleagues, but that's a whole different story.

Suffice it to say, children are a little more understanding if you explain your situation up front. It also means they'll probably never hear another word of the lesson—they're too busy thinking of questions to ask.

I've got some questions of my own about facial hair on men. Take the trend in stubble, for instance. It may seem sexy on screen, but how do they keep it the same length every day? And how many days does it take before the hottie look turns grungy?

I suspect that movie stars use a special trimmer to maintain their casually unshaven appearance. But doesn't that negate the whole purpose of not shaving?

This brings me back to the dilemma of the unplucked woman. Her courageous attitude is starting to grow on me.

I say if you've got it, flaunt it. ▼

WATCHING FOOTBALL

THERE ARE PLENTY of women who enjoy watching football. I'm not one of them.

But if I don't get into the spirit of football, I end up cutting myself off from my husband for a season that lasts longer than my hair color.

With this in mind, I set out to connect with Mr. Right on a deeper emotional level by watching football with him on TV. Not just any game, but his favorite college team.

This was not an easy step for me.

For years I found other pursuits in a galaxy far, far away whenever a football game was on. The relentless crowd noise, shrill whistles and endless commentary added up to the racket of a low-level riot in our living room. The only part I enjoyed was the marching bands at halftime, which they don't even show any more.

It wasn't always like this, searching for common ground to share with my husband.

When we were dating, our interests seemed compatible. Only later did we realize that our relationship was based on pretense: I pretended to like sports and he pretended to like conversation.

So you can imagine why, after thirty years of marriage, it was time to take another stab at finding a mutual activity.

Game day came and I gave it a try. Part of the challenge was sitting down long enough to watch the whole game. If there's such a thing as adult-onset ADD, I must have it.

I filed my nails during the first quarter and folded the laundry during the second, which still left two more hours to go. I dozed through the third quarter, then snacked my way through the final period. Sheer torture disguised as the favorite American pastime—or was that baseball?

Baseball—now there's a game that's so slow, you can't tell if your TiVo screen is on play or pause.

But don't get me started on TiVo. It's just another diabolical weapon in men's hands to make a three-hour game last for six. How many times does a person have to see each play? And why does the surround-sound bass need to levitate me from my seat? It must be a guy thing.

Speaking of guys, my husband meanwhile whooped and hollered and enjoyed the game unhindered by my presence.

"Where's my other shirt?" he called out when our team fell behind.

Convinced that his personal garb controlled the outcome of the game, he changed and rechanged his clothes. Miraculously, our team pulled ahead in the last few seconds, a victory he aided by kneeling and beating his hat on the floor.

By the end of the game I was exhausted, yet secretly proud of my endurance and the shared experience now binding us together.

My sacrifice was not lost on him.

The next day I went to a quilt show and he insisted on coming along. Mr. Right was one of three men there. It would have been more fun to go with a girlfriend who appreciated quilts. But no—he was the selfless hero, getting in touch with his feminine side, proving his devotion to me.

Afterwards, he almost broke his arm patting himself on the back.

I think I liked it better when the lines were clearly drawn. There were his activities and my activities. I didn't like football and he didn't like quilting.

My tolerance for football is waning faster than the harvest moon. Monday night's coming and I have urgent business elsewhere.

Beam me up, Scottie. ▼

PART THREE

Winter

.

.

BLACK-AND-BLUE FRIDAY

I'M NOT MUCH of a shopper, but I don't pretend to be, so it all works out.

On Black Friday this year I ventured out at 6 a.m. to battle the crowds for some UGG boot look-alikes.

The people lined up outside the store in the dark were Serious Shoppers with a capital S—highly focused, highly caffeinated shopping machines.

As the doors opened, the crowds made a beeline for the boot table with all the intensity of a military maneuver.

"Okay troops, we're going in," I mouthed into my imaginary Walkie-Talkie.

Teams of two surrounded the area and soon had stacks of boxes staked out higher than their heads. They were clearly out of my league.

You could say I'm more of a stay-at-home shopper. I'll admit to an occasional purchase from the shopping network while flipping through TV channels.

Granted, it's only been two times in ten years, but my family is starting to get concerned.

The first occasion was when I bought a hair-floofing kit. It was guaranteed to give my hair extra body and volume—extra floof. My kids made so much fun of me that I never even took it out of the box.

"Gee, Mom, we can't believe you bought something off the TV," they said. "You must be desperate."

I had better success with my second purchase. The minute I saw

Grandpa's Weeder, I knew I had to have it. It would change my life.

Imagine a tool that saves your arms, saves your back and plucks weeds all in one smooth stroke. How could I go wrong?

The demonstration seemed too good to be true. Insert the tip of the weeder, push down with your foot, and gently lean it to the side. *Voilá*, the weed is gone. I watched it several times, carefully searching for some hidden trick. Was it fake dirt? Fake weeds? So simple, yet so inspired, I couldn't afford to pass it up.

Not wanting to make an impulse purchase, I jotted down the number and waited 24 hours before calling. Of course by that time, they were all sold out.

"Fine, put me on back order," I said.

When the miracle tool finally arrived, I was happier than a carbohydrate at an Atkins diet clinic. The box alone was worth the price of the tool. Measuring 4 feet long by 1 foot wide, it was the perfect size to mail someone a set of ski poles for Christmas.

And the tool itself? It's the soul of genius. I took it out in the backyard for a test run.

"Where'd you get that?" asked my husband.

"Nunya," I replied, as in "none of your business."

"Can you show me how it works?"

He couldn't fool me—I knew he was just trying to get me to do the weeding. But 20 weeds later, he was begging to try it himself. I should have saved it for his birthday.

Last week I again succumbed to the thrill of the hunt. I ordered our Thanksgiving dinner online from Boston Market, a meal guaranteed to please.

I offered to make pies from scratch. "Aw, Mom," my kids said, "We wanted pies from Costco."

Was I insulted? Not on your life. We had a delicious meal with no fuss and no muss. It was the perfect way to give me more time for giving thanks—and watching QVC. ▼

BOXES

I'M A BOX lover from way back.

My mother and grandmother before me were box hoarders, so I come by the trait honestly.

I hesitate to call it an addiction, but it definitely borders on a compulsion.

Any box of any size that enters the portals of our house gets squirreled away for such a time as the holidays, when parcels for wrapping and mailing are at a premium. I also save large envelopes and bubble wrap, but let's not get into that right now.

During December my innate pack-rat qualities pay off handsomely when it's time to get all those packages in the mail.

Keeping the stockpile is not as easy as it sounds, because my husband limits my storage area. He doles out one measly garage cabinet where I'm allowed to feed my fetish. Like a set of Russian nesting dolls, I have to stack my boxes one inside the other just to squeeze them into the cupboard.

And that cabinet sometimes houses spiders.

You may think I'm obsessive, but where do the neighbors come when they need a box? To me, the queen of containers. They know they can count on me to have exactly the right size and shape on hand. I'll even shake out the spiders at no extra charge.

My carton craving extends to tins as well. There isn't a tin around that I haven't snagged for my collection. I can't bring myself to throw away even an Altoids can, which explains why there's a tall stack of them in an upper cabinet that falls out on anyone who opens the door.

As a child I loved to play in giant appliance boxes, so I made sure to pass on this treat to my own kids. Trains, trucks or tree houses—you could fashion them all from cardboard. Shoe boxes were a special delight, full of possibilities for making a diorama or housing your valentines.

At holidays or birthdays, my family carefully saved each box, bow and piece of wrapping paper and folded it away for the next occasion—a habit I perpetuated when Mr. Right and I got married, but which backfired on me four years later.

In 1980, after living for three years on the east coast, I moved to Escondido ahead of my husband to start a new job. Two months later, he rented a truck and drove back to California with all our worldly goods inside. Upon arriving, he hit me with a triple-header of bad news.

"Honey, I broke the corner off the living room mirror," he confessed. No problem, I could handle it.

"The lawn mower blade cut into the leg of your grandmother's antique sideboard," he added. Oh well, that could be repaired.

"And I had to throw away all the wrapping paper because it was mildewed."

That's when I broke down and wept. My precious hoard gone in an instant.

My kids love to torment me each Christmas by tearing off the wrapping paper, wadding it up and hurling it across the room.

"Hey Mom, are you saving this piece?" they taunt as they pepper each other with paper missiles.

Since I'm outnumbered by a brood of rebels and wasters, the best I can do is rescue the boxes and bows before they get crushed.

At least I'm easy to buy for. Whatever you want to give me is fine; all I really care about is the box. ▼

IT'S PUZZLING

HOLIDAY TIME AND it's time to break out a jigsaw puzzle.

I come from a long line of puzzle fans. In my family growing up, it wasn't a real holiday unless there was a puzzle in progress on a card table—the bigger and more challenging, the better.

If we had been portrayed on a TV show, you'd see a jolly scene with harmonious family members gathered around a table, laughing and talking and sharing a common goal in a cozy, fire-warmed living room. At least that's how it goes in my sugarcoated memory.

Now that I have my own, I'm afraid I've raised a puzzle-dysfunctional family.

Only one out of my three kids turned out to be a puzzler, and he peaked out in kindergarten. The other two hover around the table pretending to encourage me, meanwhile surreptitiously hiding a piece so they can be the one to put the last piece in. Where did I go wrong?

My husband's clan brings a new wrinkle into the process. With them it's a territorial dispute. Woe to you if you get in the way of the flying fingers. Add a diverse mix of personalities, stir well and watch things bubble over. I've found it best to step *awaaaaay* from the table.

I've given up working puzzles with Mr. Right because of his irritating habit of tapping his finger three times loudly on the piece he's just inserted. Tap-tap-tap. Look-at-me, he raps in Morse code.

"Good job, Honey," I say brightly.

Get over it, I'm thinking. There are 999 more pieces to go. He must have a deep need for more attention. Either that, or he was weaned too early. I spend more time on congratulating him than looking for the next piece.

To be fair, I have to add that after reading this, he said I've got it all wrong.

"I do it just to annoy you," he said.

Call me antisocial, but puzzling has become a solo activity for me. It's a good pastime when you're supposed to be taking it easy. In fact, it's become so addictive that I've done three 1000-piecers in the last couple weeks.

You'd think that assembling a puzzle would be a relatively safe activity, but come to find out, it has its own hidden hazards. When I went to the chiropractor complaining of a crippling pain in my rear end, I received some discouraging news.

"It's from too much sitting," the chiropractor said.

Too much sitting? It's not as if I'm up to kayaking or running marathons these days.

I also enjoy solving the Cryptoquote and Jumble in the newspaper. I heard that mental exercise can help to keep your brain young, so I take my daily dose of puzzles as faithfully as my vitamins.

My husband, on the other hand, prefers to do the Sudoku, which shouldn't surprise me because he was on the math team in high school. I tried it once and had about as much success as I did in algebra class.

But that's okay. To each his own when it comes to puzzles.

One time we saw an elderly couple sitting together in McDonald's eating breakfast and silently doing their crosswords side by side.

"Isn't that cute," said my husband. "That could be us when we get old."

It may not be exactly what I had in mind for our golden years, but I do hope we'll still be working puzzles.

Now if I can figure out a way to do them standing up. ▼

COOKING UP CHRISTMAS

I DON'T KNOW what came over me.

The picture looked so scrumptious in the magazine—my only defense for why I attempted to make something new for Christmas dinner last year.

And while I'm confessing, make that two new recipes on one holiday. This from a person who hasn't tried any new recipes for several years.

Maybe it was the influence of my friend Donna, who cooks up something innovative several times a week. Or perhaps it was a case of temporary insanity brought on by the mouth-watering photos in the magazine.

Possibly my judgment was clouded by the double-barreled wad of Kleenex stuffed into my nostrils to halt the flow of a runny nose. My winter cold hadn't gotten the memo to turn off the faucet.

In any event, it was the night before Christmas and I was in the kitchen, assembling the ingredients for Salt-Encrusted Prime Rib of Beef. How hard could it be? I felt confident in my ability to read a recipe, follow instructions and work the timer.

Fast-forward to the next day. I'm not saying that the dish was a failure. It smelled delicious. The gorgeous, brown crust of kosher salt and fresh rosemary sprigs made an impressive sight as it fractured and fell off to one side, right on cue.

So what was the problem? Let's just say it was a bit under-cooked.

It's possible that the reading on the meat thermometer was obscured by decades of old stains covering the numbers. It's also possible that the words "medium rare" on the recipe actually meant "barely dead" in some other universe.

I probably should have taken the cooking time and doubled it, as you would with estimates for home remodeling projects.

Whatever the reason, after bravely slicing the bloody beef with the electric carving knife, my husband sent the still-shuddering pieces into the microwave for a refresher course in edibility.

"It's okay," he reassured me. "We'll just cook it some more."

After such a sight it was a little difficult to eat. Visions of ultra-rare roast beef dancing in your head make for a good appetite suppressant.

My theory is that meat always tastes better when someone else cooks it because you haven't seen it raw. Not to mention peeling that lovely absorbent layer off the bottom of the package. Who thought up sanitary pads for meat, anyway?

Jumping ahead to dessert time, I had found the Cheesecake Brownie recipe in the newspaper right next to a coupon for cream cheese. Again, the picture said it all. What could be more tempting than chewy, chocolate brownies topped with a scrumptious layer of chocolate chip cheesecake?

In hindsight, my first hint of disaster should have been when the recipe called for a sheet of foil to line the baking pan. It sounded like an efficient way to serve the dessert. But once again, the cooking time was grossly underestimated.

It took two people and four hands to lever the foil up from the cooking dish. "On my count," I said, heaving it out of the pan like doctors lifting a patient on a medical show.

Like a prehistoric landform shifting under subterranean stress, the dessert cracked down the middle and unleashed a glacier of uncooked chocolate ooze. We stuck a spoon in it and called it pudding.

There's a reason why recipes are tried and true. Untried and untrue is the flip side of that coin, I now realize. You can bet this year I'll be sticking with the old favorites. ▼

MEMORY AIDS

IT'S A GOOD thing that Tuesday is trash day in our neighborhood so I can remember to put it out on the right morning. Operative clue? The letter T.

I feel sorry for those who live in the Monday, Wednesday or Friday trash zones. Or maybe you feel sorrier for me because I need such a method for remembering things.

Which reminds me: on the weeks when there's a holiday on Monday, have you ever wondered when the extra day's trash gets picked up? As far as I can tell, the trash collectors are already working at top speed. It boggles the mind.

Sad to say, I'm reduced to using memory aids more and more. There was a time when I could turn my watch around or change my ring to another finger if I needed a reminder, but even those old tried-and-true methods are failing faster than the glue on the back of an old sticky note.

Recently I was distressed to find myself out in public fully dressed, but wearing only one earring. I was afraid I'd lost the other one.

My husband tried to reassure me. "You could always wear it with the mate from the last one you lost," he said.

But I was still worried. I hurried home and found the missing earring on the bathroom counter right where I'd left it. Relief gave way to dismay as I realized that I'd simply forgotten to put it on.

Developing a strategy is crucial. And what better way to aid recall than using the days of the week?

As a child I always wished for a set of days-of-the-week

underwear. I wondered if people really wore them on the right day or if anyone ever checked, like the panty police.

Would you stack them up in the drawer and take them off the top of the heap? Or maybe keep them in a handy seven-day organizer, like the purple container my husband gave me for my pills. (Now there's a gift you don't know whether to be excited or insulted about.)

What if the days of the week were named after something else, like the Seven Dwarfs? You'd have a good excuse for being sleepy, sneezy, happy or dopey once a week. Doc-day would be the perfect time to schedule all those doctor's appointments.

I'm usually okay in the morning once I figure out which day it is.

In my system, each day has its letter-coordinated tasks. For instance, on Wednesdays there's watering and winding the clock, weeding and writing—a regular smorgasbord of W-chores.

Fridays are for fun, since my column appears in the paper. And Saturdays are for sleeping in. You can see why I never get around to ironing or cleaning—no days start with I or C.

I still haven't devised a way to remember hair-washing day. It's tricky because I like to wash my hair every other day, but there's an uneven number of days in a week. Maybe I should get a 14-day dial set to go off every two days like the lawn sprinklers.

You'd think somebody would invent a facial recognition memory aid. Unlike a hearing aid, it wouldn't squeal and drive you crazy. A tiny camera would scan an incoming person's face and whisper their name just in time for you to say hello—a job my husband currently does for me.

Thank goodness for all the gadgets that help to find misplaced items. I love car keys that chirp when you clap your hands and phones that beep when you press the locator.

Next I'll have to look for a set of beeping earrings. ▼

NEW YEAR'S RESOLUTIONS I DIDN'T MAKE

IT'S SAID THAT not to decide is to decide. If the same holds true at New Year's, then not to resolve is to resolve.

I have a whole list of resolutions I didn't make this year.

Lose weight. I figure if I haven't lost it by now, I'm not going to lose it by the usual methods. Fixating on food just makes me want to eat more of it, so I plan to fool myself by pretending I'm not trying to take off the pounds.

It's amusing to watch the annual cycle of over-indulgence at the holidays turn into a January frenzy of weight-loss articles in magazines and introductory specials at the gym. TV commercials follow suit. I guess everybody except me must have resolved to lose weight.

Eat better. I'm not going to do that either. After all my years of avoiding hamburgers and French fries and exercising regularly, I still had a heart attack. From now on I'm letting the medications work their magic in my arteries.

Decorate the Christmas tree. Never again. Things worked out fine this year with an unadorned tree. When my kids had their annual wrapping paper battle, the wads and bows landed on the branches and looked quite festive as recycled ornaments.

Clean the house more often. And rob myself of the joy of receiving a love letter, "I ♥ U," written in hair on the shower wall? Not on your life. I wouldn't want to curb my husband's creativity any more than I'd want to strain my back scrubbing.

I didn't see the message at first, but when Mr. Right called from the office to ask if I'd showered yet, I knew something was up. I wrote back with hair on the wall, "Me2." Too bad the message dried up and fell off by the next day. I guess I'll still need to buy him a Valentine's card this year.

Talk with my son more. That's a joke. Son Two came and sat down next to me while I was writing this column and tried to get my attention. I lifted my chin to acknowledge him and went back to work. Next he smacked the arm of my chair. I took out my earplugs and asked, "Do you want to talk?"

"No," he said. "Do you want to toast me a bagel?"

"No," I replied.

See, we already communicate perfectly.

You may think that my non-resolutions are really resolutions by default. I admit they smack a little of reverse psychology.

Our Favorite Dotter picked up on the idea of reverse psychology at an early age. It worked well for a while. We could get her to do whatever we wanted by telling her not to do it. But soon the light dawned.

"Hey, you're reverse psychologing me," she complained, before she even knew how to pronounce the words.

"If you can't say it, you're too young to know about it," we replied.

It was a sad day when she figured out our parental strategy. From then on we had to use reverse-reverse psychology, which proved to be confusing. It took more effort on our part, but at least it made her stop and think a little longer. And she learned how to outsmart us, a skill that prepared her well for the teen years.

Maybe I am deceiving myself with my anti-resolution stance. But by refusing to make the perennial list, I bypassed the whole tedious cycle of resolving, failing and trying again.

Now I can relax and enjoy the new year. ▼

THE SPAY BUS

THE HUM OF a special event filled the school parking lot. Balloons flying, signs flapping, coffee urns flowing, orange-vested volunteers directing traffic—all the excitement of an outdoor festival.

Where did this whirl of activity come from, I wondered as I walked down a street that's usually quiet on Saturday mornings. Cars lined up, dogs frolicked in the backs of pickup trucks and a carnival atmosphere reigned.

Then I rounded the corner and saw the reason why. The Spay Bus had come to town.

I'm not kidding. There really is a vehicle called the Spay Bus—or the Neuter Scooter—depending upon which one comes to a neighborhood near you. Designed as an economical way to curb the propagation of unwanted pets, I believe it's a concept whose time has come.

I wish they'd had something similar years ago when it was time for my kids to be immunized.

"Hey kids, let's go for a ride on the bus!" It would have saved all the weeping and wailing and gnashing of teeth that occurred when they found out we were headed to the doctor for their shots.

Many companies already provide portable services. There's mobile car detailing, windshield repair and pet groomers who come right to your door.

Think of the other services that could follow suit.

Move over, Bloodmobile. Make way for the Vasectomy Van. It's the perfect solution for all those reluctant husbands who promised their wives they'd have the procedure, but never got around to scheduling the appointment.

"Here, Honey, I've got a free ticket for you." I can picture it now.

I felt a bit sorry for the unsuspecting pets who thought they were going on a special outing. It could scar them for life, or at least make them skittish about boarding busses.

It's almost as bad as some of the trickery I used when my kids were small. When we were at the park and the ice cream truck came by, I didn't want Son One begging me for a treat, so I told him it was a music truck.

Technically speaking, it wasn't a lie. It was a partial truth.

I'll never forget the time he came running up with the light of discovery in his eyes and said, "Mom! Guess what *else* is inside the music truck."

You may think my mothering methods were cruel and unusual, but I meant well.

I felt bad recently when Son One, now 23, mentioned that the music truck was playing a new song in his neighborhood. Everyone laughed at his choice of words, and I had to take the blame.

But I was not alone. He and Son Two joined in perpetrating another innocent scam on their baby sister. They convinced her that the bruise on the banana was extra sweet, the most coveted part.

"Give her the bruise," they would say, and she thought she was getting special treatment.

A little harmless deception merely ensures that our kids will have fodder for future years of psychotherapy. Someday they'll write a best-seller about how horribly they were treated.

Can you imagine the books those newly neutered pets could write?

But if dogs could read, they wouldn't be caught dead near the spay bus in the first place. You might have to disguise it as a toy store.

Watch out the next time you go into Spays "R" Us. ▼

DIRECTIONALLY CHALLENGED

YOU'VE HEARD OF people who can't find their way out of a paper bag? I might not be that bad, but I admit to being directionally challenged.

Okay, I'll be honest. It's not just a slight case of confusion, but a deep-seated syndrome bordering on a malady. Soon they'll be making a special license plate for my condition.

Although my chronic affliction lies dormant most of the time, it flared up last week when I drove to the newspaper office in San Marcos, where they wanted to take a new picture for my column. (This was before the days of smart phones and mobile apps.) The directions online were out of date and the photographer assured me it was much easier to use the new freeway exit.

Four wrong turns, two phone calls and two stops to ask directions later, I arrived at my destination, which turned out to be only two blocks away from the freeway.

My editor was puzzled. "Didn't you come here once before?" he asked, as if that should have inoculated me against getting lost.

"Yes, but that was a few months ago," I said.

Some people can find their way back to a location after being there once, but not me. I must have missed out on the homing-pigeon gene.

My directional disorder is so pervasive that I've started thinking of it as a talent. After all, what are the odds that a person could turn the wrong direction 100 percent of the time? Any other person would have a 50-50 chance to get it right, but I have an uncanny knack for going the wrong way every time.

The problem isn't only when I'm driving.

One time I got lost inside Kmart and started crying. Fortunately my husband found me a few minutes later and all was well. And you thought this was an incident from my childhood.

At least it provides some amusement for him. Mr. Right loves it when I get out of an elevator and take off down the hall going the wrong way. He hangs back and waits for me to go first so I can't see the smirk on his face.

Putting a fitted sheet on the mattress is a similar trial. No matter which corner I start with, the second one is always wrong. That's why I believe it must be a gift.

Cute memory chants can take you only so far in life. "Righty-tighty, lefty-loosy" is my favorite maxim for screwing in a light bulb. And the instructions for making a square knot: Right over left and left over right. Or was that vice versa? Knot tying is a lost art anyway.

As for map reading, I have a checkered past. My husband gave up asking me to navigate after the time I used his favorite book map for a placemat. When I rolled down the window to shake off the crumbs, the whole page tore off and blew away.

Someone has said, "Men read maps better than women because only men can understand the concept of an inch equaling a hundred miles." I think they have a point.

Shortly after my "cardiac event," I wished aloud that someone would give me a road map to get through the next few months of recovery.

"You couldn't read it if you had one," said Mr. Right—not exactly the comfort I was looking for.

Let's hope my next car comes equipped with a built-in GPS system and a kindly woman's voice to direct me when I'm lost.

I bet she could help me with the bed sheets, too. ▼

THIS LITTLE PIGGY STAYED HOME

I DON'T KNOW many people who like their toes.

Except for my husband, who thinks his are perfect, and little kids, who love playing "This Little Piggy," lots of people have toe issues.

Everyone has different reasons for disliking their toes.

My friend Jeanne is repulsed by the fact that her second toe is longer than the first. She thinks it's a deformity, a prehensile appendage left over from the days of the dinosaurs. The more she talks about it, the more you want to rip her shoes off and take a look.

Then there's the family member who suffers from an aversion to naked feet. An entire movie outing can be ruined for this person by sitting behind someone who has their bare feet up on the back of a theater seat.

Another relative has a toe that's curled underneath the other toes, so he's gone through life with deep-seated insecurities.

Of course, I have my own hang-ups. The last time I showed my feet in public was when I was 18. I had just started dating Mr. Right when he commented on my short, stubby toes.

"They look like Tater Tots," he said.

This was back in the 1970s when the crispy potato cylinders were the most coveted section of the TV dinners our family ate on Friday nights. But I didn't take it as a compliment.

You can be sure that I never again ate a Tater Tot or went barefoot for that matter. Scarred for life? You betcha. It took me a long time to work up the nerve to get a pedicure. I was afraid the beautician would say, "Sorry, we don't do Tater Tots."

Speaking of pedicures, I'm a little scared of those foot-smoothing tools. Someone recently gave me a four-sided foot care paddle that has a metal grater on one side. Who's going to scrape that against her foot? It's bad enough when you grate your knuckles into the cheddar cheese. I'm not about to allow a metal rasp anywhere near my toes.

To be fair, not all toes get bad press. Some people are proud of their digits. I have a childhood friend who can wave her right pinkie toe without moving the others. She named it her Hello Toe, at least that's what we called it in sixth grade.

There are also people who can perform incredible skills with their toes. I've heard of individuals drawing, writing and even changing a baby's diaper with their toes—a real feat, no pun intended.

I remember as a kid sitting up in bed trying to use my toes as a book holder. Cramping set in and I soon gave up. Such a skill would come in handy these days for those whose arms aren't quite long enough to read a menu. I'm not naming names, but my new pocket-sized lighted magnifier might be useful the next time we go out to eat.

It could be worse. Mr. Right could have said my toes looked like Hostess Twinkies or cocktail wieners. At least he picked something cute and compact for the comparison.

You can imagine that 35 years later he regrets ever saying anything in the first place.

Maybe it's time to boost my toes' self-esteem.

I don't want to hear those piggies crying "Wee, wee, wee" all the way home. ▼

WHO TRIED IT FIRST?

ANOTHER BATCH OF "ponderisms" recently made its way around the Internet with such burning questions as: Is gruntled the opposite of disgruntled? And: Why do men have nipples?

I have my own list of items to ponder. Most of them speculate about who pioneered new ideas. Here are some things I wonder about.

Who first tried to eat an artichoke?

It must have been an act of bravery—or lunacy. Its sharp leaves and barbed petals make it one of the more off-putting plants in the garden. Imagine cutting it, boiling it and scraping off the "meat" (euphemism for a light green shadow) with your teeth for the first time.

And have you ever gotten a piece of the thistle in your mouth by mistake? After such an experience, I wonder who was bold enough to dig past the choke and reach the heart.

Maybe it all started with a dare: "I dare you to eat that pinecone."

"I double-dare you to eat that artichoke."

"First one to the middle wins."

"I'm putting peanut butter on mine."

"Forget peanuts, I'm putting butter on mine.

Eating artichokes proves my theory that people will eat anything if it's dipped in melted butter.

Who first charged another person for a piece of land?

In the Garden of Eden, I doubt there was a price on the ground beneath Adam and Eve's bare feet.

Somewhere in the history of the planet, somebody hatched an idea that the earth under his tent, shack or cave was personal property. And he talked someone else into paying him for it.

You've got to hand it to that person for his sales skills. Taking a section of dirt, building a fence around it, and sticking a "for sale" sign on the corner was a stroke of genius. It all paid off handsomely in the end. Just look at the real estate values along the coast.

Who first rubbed a pumice stone on her heels?

I got a pumice stone with a nice handle for Christmas and it started me thinking. Why would anyone grab a boulder and start scraping it on her feet in the first place?

Maybe it goes back to prehistoric days when people sat around scratching themselves with rocks and sticks. Where do you find pumice? And how did they settle on that particular type of rock? The trial-and-error part of the discovery must have been painful.

"Hey Wilma, let's use that volcanic rock to soften our feet."

"No thanks, Betty. I already tried the granite and it made me bleed. You try the pumice."

Who first called a mouth a "pie hole"?

Last week I tried to get my husband to be quiet by telling him to shut his cake hole. He died laughing as he corrected me. Cake hole, pie hole donut hole—what's the diff? Who's to say which is right or wrong? I want to know who made him the word police.

Who first shaved his face?

I suppose it was only a matter of time before early man tried to rid himself of facial hair. But I wonder how many sharp objects he discarded before inventing a razor blade to do the job?

After watching "The Flintstones" as a kid, I have to surmise that it was all a woman's idea. And I bet she tried out the pumice stone on him first. ▼

FRIENDSHIP BREAD

DELIVER ME FROM friendship bread.

It's not that I spurn friendship or that I despise bread. But if you're talking about the creeping, crawling bowls of sourdough starter that live and breed on kitchen countertops across the country, I have to draw the line.

During the 1980s friendship bread was a popular fad. The basic premise was that you got a batch of starter from a friend and grew it for 10 days, adding the proper ingredients at prescribed intervals.

Then, on day 10, you baked a cake or bread or muffins with part of the dough and gave them as a gift to a friend. You'd also pass on a batch of the starter, keeping a portion for yourself, thus perpetuating another cycle.

You can imagine the pressures involved. Day 10 didn't always fall at a convenient time for baking, but the dough was relentless; it kept marching on. Like a mad science experiment, it demanded constant attention to keep it in check.

And if you weren't careful, the foaming, fermenting mass of bubbles took on a life of its own.

Around this same time, recipe chains became popular among the stay-at-home-mom crowd. You never knew when you'd get a piece of mail asking you to send the letter on to six friends. They would send it to six friends, and you'd magically get 36 recipes in the mail. Not that any young mother has time to try 36 new recipes.

In reality, nobody could ever think of six people to pass the letter on to. This was a real test of friendship—a pain in the neck which, to my knowledge, never made it past the first link before somebody broke the chain.

And all this before the days of forwarding email on the Internet.

But back to friendship bread.

The dough came with precise directions. One of them was never to put a batch of starter in a sealed container, a piece of advice I didn't take very seriously—until one Sunday.

It was Day 10 and I was rushing off to church. I can get rid of the dough there, I thought. Surely some unsuspecting friend will take it off my hands. So I slapped the glob into an empty plastic butter tub and snapped on the lid.

My duties at church kept me behind the piano, which was onstage to the right of the podium. I stacked my parcels behind the piano to be retrieved after the service and played the opening songs, after which I went down to sit in the audience.

Midway through the sermon, there was a loud report from the front of the church. Ba-BAM! The pastor, my husband, jumped back, thinking he'd been shot. He looked around, but couldn't see anything amiss. No blood, so he went on.

At the end of the service I went up to the piano to play the closing song, and all became clear. The plastic dough container had exploded, leaving splatters of sticky goo oozing all over the piano and the carpet.

Never again did I try to pass off a batch of friendship dough. We ate the last round of cake and purged our house of all traces of starter, like a Jewish mother sweeping the house clean before Passover.

A few months later, a visiting relative came bearing friendship bread starter as a hostess gift.

I smiled sweetly and thanked her, but the minute she left, I slam-dunked it into the trash can.

It was small price to pay to preserve our friendship. ▼

30-MINUTE BLADDER

HOW FAR CAN you go on a 30-minute bladder?

This is a mileage calculation that most women of a certain age can do instantly in their heads.

In my case, it depends upon whether I am sitting or standing. If I'm sitting, I can go for an hour or two without a bathroom break. Otherwise, it's every 30 minutes on the average. Any activity longer than an hour demands careful planning to dehydrate myself.

If you have a bladder the size of an acorn, you learn to make adjustments in life. You scout out every restroom along your route and you know how to get to it quickly.

Our kids grew up thinking that all tourists visit the bathroom first. They think it's normal to stop at every restroom within a one-mile radius of your destination. They think it's cool to take the one-hour white-water river rafting trip instead of the four-hour version.

When my husband and I traveled to England a few years back, I was delighted to discover that judges there give out Loo of the Year awards to worthy public bathrooms. In fact, I planned my itinerary around a tour of all the prizewinning potties.

Here in the U.S. we use euphemisms such as restroom, ladies' lounge, powder room or bath room, but in England they tell it like it is: toilet. The signs are clear. All except for the time when I saw a sign proclaiming: "To let." Thinking that a letter was missing, I hurried over to use the facilities, but it turned out to be a room for rent.

My husband, on the other hand, is blessed with a heroic capacity for holding his water. When they were handing out bladders he must have said, "Supersize me." And since opposites always marry, you can guess there's been some friction along the way.

He's one of those guys who, in the early days of our family vacations, believed in starting a road trip with the gas tank full and the bladders empty, and didn't stop until the opposite was true.

Now that we have one grown offspring who inherited my tiny bladder, I have more help lobbying for bathroom stops along the road. But in the early days when the kids were young, it was a different story.

There were times when all I wished for was a Porta-Potty on wheels that we could haul behind the minivan.

One trip stands out. The kids were ages 5, 3 and 1, and we were driving up the California coast to visit friends near Morro Bay. Mr. Right was slated to speak at a church on the weekend, so he brought his suit and hung it inside the van.

Shortly after a scheduled rest stop, our 3-year-old son suddenly had to go to the bathroom again. Nature called, but the husband wasn't stopping.

"Why don't you just have him pee into the empty Coke bottle?" he suggested.

Feeling none too happy about it, I clambered to the back and jammed the 2-liter bottle into place. Son Two started going, and all went well until we hit a bump in the road. Bodies shifted and parts became disengaged from the bottle. That's when he began to spray the car.

What could have been a disaster turned into a case of poetic justice. This was a kid with good aim. He had hosed the front of his dad's suit.

Now my husband and I are both older and wiser. When I say, "Pull over," he says, "How soon?"

I don't even have to wave a Coke bottle to get my way. ▼

WEATHER WIMPS

THEY CALL US weather wimps.

We're the Southern California residents whom the rest of the country scorns for being spoiled by our mild climate.

While people in other states stock up on beans and franks, candles and matches, water and batteries, in San Diego County we check our supplies of suntan lotion and sport drinks.

I'm not asking for pity, just a little understanding. It's a big day for us when the breeze kicks up or the temperature drops below 50. A few drops of rain can make our month, and when there were snow flurries in Malibu recently, you'd think it was a national holiday.

The closest we ever get to a blizzard is buying dessert at the local Dairy Queen.

Because we don't have many weather changes, we have to make them up to fill the evening news. I mean, how many different ways can you say sunny and warm? And since the leaves on most of our trees don't turn, we are thrilled by the slightest variation.

The other morning I looked out my kitchen window and got excited when I saw the tree next door had changed color. Okay, so it was covered with toilet paper, but any alteration can elevate the heart rate.

Transplanted southern Californians are bound to suffer some embarrassment when they move to snowy parts of the country. During our first winter living in Philadelphia, my husband was eager to buy a snow shovel.

After the first snowstorm, he stood out in the street, leaning on his shovel, admiring the expanse of driveway he had just cleared—

side to side and the full length—when a neighbor came out to chat.

"You're not from around here, are you?" commented the neighbor.

"How could you tell?" asked Mr. Right.

"Because you cleared the whole driveway," he said. "But you'll learn."

And we did. First of all, you make sure to find a house with a flat driveway. Second, you park at the end closest to the street. Third, you dig out only the exact width of your car. They should have given us a manual when we crossed the Pennsylvania border.

But the biggest thrill was getting snow days off from school. We hovered around the radio in the mornings, holding our breath to catch our school number on the list of school closings.

This was before we had kids, so the breathless student was actually Mr. Right, who was going to grad school at the time. He was just as tickled to get out of school as the rest of the kids on the block.

I guess the more it costs to attend, the happier you are when it's called off. No matter that the rest of the time we were pinching pennies to save on heating oil.

Our house was so cold that we bundled up to sit in our own living room. Instead of heating the house, we wore Snug Sacks, clever sleeping bag–like garments that zipped up the front and snapped around the shoulders to form little outlets for our mittened hands.

The problem came when the phone rang—in the days before portable phones, answering machines or cell phones—and neither of us wanted to get up to answer it. You couldn't walk in a Snug Sack, so we took turns pogo-sticking over to the phone and answering it with our protruding flippers.

Maybe that's why we appreciate California weather so much.

We've retired our Snug Sacks, and whenever we get a case of blizzard envy, it's a short drive to the nearest Dairy Queen. ▼

PART FOUR

Spring

Lois Swagerty

MOST EMBARRASSING MOMENTS

I COLLECT EMBARRASSING moments the way Imelda Marcos collected shoes.

Over the years some of my moments have become legendary. If conversation at a party is lagging, it always helps to break out the old tales and tell them again. You can't beat them as ice breakers for the sheer horror they conjure up.

My two most unforgettable incidents took place about 30 years ago. At least I can claim that I've matured some since then.

It was my first job after college and I worked in the marketing department of a surgical instrument company in Fort Washington, Pennsylvania. The company made a variety of tools, including trachea tubes.

My desk was situated right around the corner from the lobby, and often I could hear what went on at the reception desk.

One day I heard a fascinating sound coming from the other side of the wall. It was sort of a twanging, musical tone that had me up and out of my seat faster than you could say "Oh Brother, Where Art Thou."

As I rounded the corner I asked the receptionist, "Who's playing the Jew's harp!"—a mouth instrument I'd always been curious to see up close.

It was an instrument all right, but not the one I imagined. A client who'd had his larynx removed was vocalizing by holding a vibrating machine against his neck. The receptionist tried to wave me off, but it was too late.

I don't remember what happened next, only the effort of trying to become invisible.

The second incident occurred in the same setting. This time I was circulating around the office, returning to my desk by way of the lobby. Two coworkers filed through the office ahead of me. Suddenly I noticed that all three of us were wearing black outfits. We could have been a singing group, we were so color coordinated.

"What is this—*black* day?" I asked.

Just then our little parade hit the lobby where two African-American women sat filling out job applications.

Since then I've learned to look before I leap, or at least before I speak.

But humiliation still happens. Case in point took place only a few years back while riding my bicycle down Carlsbad Village Drive toward the beach.

Somehow I forgot that I wasn't driving a car, and thought I could shoot the yellow light. By the time I pedaled wildly through, the light had long since turned red.

"Lady on the bike, pull over!" came the magnified words from a police microphone.

I was busted. The thought of having to go home and admit my misdeed to my husband and three teenage drivers was more than I could face. So I did the only honorable thing. I cried.

The officer let me off with a warning, but the experience of running a red light on my bike—and getting caught—still stings. I finally confessed it to my incredulous family, a decision I've come to regret.

I'm surprised that more people don't share their embarrassing stories.

To quote a line from the song "The Way We Were," I guess "what's too painful to remember, we simply choose to forget." ▼

PURSE VERSUS BACKPACK

TO PURSE OR to backpack—that is the question.

For some women, their choice is all about image. For me, it's all about function, and I don't mean feng shui. I've recently become a backpack convert after more than 40 years of faithful purse carrying.

The only drawback I find with wearing a backpack is the tendency to whack unsuspecting people standing in line behind you, unless you also count knocking pricey items off the shelves in tiny boutiques. I don't deny that caution is needed.

When I tried to switch back to a shoulder bag recently, I found it impossible. Somewhere along the way I became a slave to the sly charm of a backpack: hoisting more stuff with less strain.

It used to be that backpacks were the domain of the hip, trendy crowd. But as with any other fashion, they jumped the shark when middle-aged women put them on.

My version isn't even one of those stylish, sporty packs. It's a hybrid on straps or backpurse—a label I've coined that's sure to catch on.

Handbags have always been about security. Something in women's genetic makeup dictates that we can't leave home without bringing more supplies than a rescue expedition in the Andes.

I trace it back to watching "Let's Make a Deal" on TV at an early age. When Monty Hall popped into the audience at the end of the show and paid cash for bizarre items found in ladies' purses, he inspired me to a lifetime of eternal readiness.

Never again would I be caught without having a whole lemon or a cancelled stamp stashed in my satchel, just to be safe.

And satchel is right. If you want to be prepared, you have to be willing to heft the weight. No little fanny packs for me. My dream purse was a Mary Poppins–like—a magical carpet bag that could hold a coat tree with no noticeable bulge.

During my purse-carrying years, I once owned a sweet leather model with a light inside that turned on automatically when you opened the top.

It was the best thing since lights in refrigerators. No more groping around in darkened theaters for Kleenex or a Junior Mint. I was so tickled, the gadget lover in me had died and gone to heaven.

Around that time I developed a problem with one of my credit cards which kept failing after only a few weeks of use. The third time I called to order a new one, I mentioned the recurring trouble to the customer service representative on the phone.

She got very quiet. "May I ask you a question about your purse?"

"Okay." Here it comes, I thought. Finally, a prize for my purse contents.

"Do you have a magnet in your purse?" she asked.

"Sorry, I don't."

"Well, if you did, it could be ruining your credit card," she explained.

Then it hit me. My purse light was triggered by a magnetic clasp. It had to be the culprit.

I ended up cutting the magnet out of the purse with an X-Acto knife, a sad little magnet-ectomy performed on the patient without benefit of anesthesia.

Although I kept the purse for a while, the thrill was gone. I reverted to looking in the fridge for excitement, and switched to carrying a backpack.

Forget about trying to make a fashion statement. The only thing my backpack says about me these days is, "This woman carries too much junk."

From here it's only one short step to a rolling duffle. ▼

CLEARING THE CLUTTER

"THIS IS NOT a garage sale," stated the sign in front of our neighbor's house.

Given the amount of things piled out in front, they were smart to post a notice. Several carloads of shoppers had already pulled up to browse.

You know you're in trouble when your driveway is so full of stuff that people drive up and start offering you cash.

In defense of the neighbors, they had been remodeling for most of a year and were finally getting things organized to move back in. So they had a good excuse for having half their household goods stacked in the driveway.

But there are plenty of other people who struggle with neatness issues. Clutter? It's merely mind over matter. If you don't mind, it doesn't matter.

Take junk drawers, for instance. Everyone has them, it's just a question of whether or not you can get them closed.

My husband, a compulsive organizer, has his tiny drawers of nuts and bolts all neatly labeled. He made diagrams of where boxes are stored in the garage rafters. We knew Son One had inherited his genes when he sorted his Legos by size and color as a child.

Then there's the other end of the spectrum.

A friend once had her van stolen. Fortunately the police were able to recover the vehicle after only a few days. But when they notified her to come retrieve it, they gave her an advance warning.

"We're sorry to report that the thieves completely trashed your car," they said.

When she went to pick it up, she found it in exactly the same condition as she'd left it. She pretended to be appalled.

Another friend's front door blew open while she was out of town. The security company came and inspected for intruders. They left a written report stating that most of the house looked unharmed except for the teenage girl's room, which had been ransacked. Did they want to file a police report?

Teenagers' bedrooms get plenty of bad press; I don't need to add to it here. I figure if I wait long enough, their own kids will come along and pay them back. It's the Circle of Life.

What I don't understand is how you can spend years training your kids to pick up things and put them away, and have it amount to zilch.

As a mother of youngsters, I perpetuated a daily tidy-up time. We made a game out of it, complete with singing "A Spoonful of Sugar Helps the Medicine Go Down."

"A place for everything, and everything in its place," was my mother's mantra. She was the kind of person who alphabetized the spices in her cupboard.

Somewhere along the way I failed miserably in passing this value on to my kids. Instead, Son Two devised his own method. Whenever he had to clean up his room, he stuffed all the junk into a jumbo trash bag and hoisted it up into the attic.

It wasn't such a bad idea when you think about it, because when we get ready to clean out the attic, everything will already be bagged for the Dumpster.

However, if we work it right, I bet we could make some money in the process. We'll stack all the bags in the driveway and wait for the cars to pull up.

Early birds welcome. ▼

DON'T LET THE BED BUGS BITE

THE OTHER MORNING I hopped out of bed, grabbed the sheets, and started to pull up the covers when I froze in horror.

There were several tiny, flat reddish-brown thingies on the bed.

Immediately I feared the worst: bed bugs! Isn't there an epidemic of the little rust-colored bloodsuckers in the United States right now? I knew I should have paid more attention to those warnings on the news.

All I could think about was armies of Pac–manlike creatures with their little mouths chewing and chewing while I was asleep.

I've never actually seen a bed bug, and to quote the poem about purple cows, I never hope to see one.

When it comes to things that go munch in the night, I'm as squeamish as the next person. It doesn't help that a voice from my childhood used to put me to bed chanting, "Good night, sleep tight; don't let the bed bugs bite."

That little rhyme ranks right up there among the top two worst sentiments to take with you to bed—the other being the traditional prayer, "Now I lay me down to sleep" which contains the alarming line, "If I should die before I wake...." Not a cheery thought when you're trying to get to sleep.

When I saw the brown specks, I calmed my breathing and tried to think rationally. If these were bed bugs, wouldn't they run and hide? And aren't they microscopic?

Come to find out, that would be skin mites, the invisible organisms that feast on sloughed off particles of skin. Another soothing thought for insomniacs.

Looking up bugs on the Internet is enough to make your skin crawl. Between the threat of scabies, skin mites and chiggers, I was ready to have my whole house fumigated.

It reminded me of Son One's house in Los Angeles where several college students lived. The occupants suffered from bites in the night that itched mercilessly and left red marks on their legs. It turns out the house was infested with pigeon mites, a facet of student life that wasn't mentioned in the handbook.

Once you start thinking about tiny insects, it's hard to stop scratching.

At springtime in elementary schools a predictable phenomenon occurs. At least once a year, usually after the chicken pox season, there's an outbreak of lice which sends everyone scurrying to the health technician to get their heads checked.

It's a fact of life and all the parents know that it could be their turn next to get the dreaded call, no matter how hygienic their home or how careful they are. Little League coaches stock up on helmet spray and parents pray they'll escape the dreaded ordeal.

Once when I was a teacher, I was so certain I was infested that I went to see the nurse on my day off. "Would you please check me for lice," I begged. "My scalp itches and I'm afraid."

After a quick exam she said, "I think you just need to wash your hair." Hard to say whether I was more relieved or more mortified.

Getting back to the specks in the bed, I gathered up my courage and put on my glasses. The objects swam into focus and took on the shape of little oblong seeds, minus the telltale legs.

Thank goodness they weren't bed bugs, only flaxseeds that had escaped through the seam of my microwaveable heating pack.

I'm still scratching, though. ▼

NO FOOL LIKE AN APRIL FOOL

APRIL FOOLS DAY is right around the corner and since it's my favorite holiday, I thought I'd pass along a few pranks from my personal collection.

It started when I was four years old. My dad tied the legs of the chairs together at the breakfast table on April Fools' Day morning and it left an indelible impression.

Fast-forward 20 years to when I worked in an office. The best tricks utilized the old-fashioned telephone, either by sticking a rubber finger on the mouthpiece to hit people in the chin, or taping down the button so it would keep on ringing after being picked up. Too bad the phones today don't have such a button.

Another classic caper required a head start. It involved moving the boss's office furniture several inches farther back each day. On April 1, he wondered why he couldn't fit behind his desk.

I'll admit, my stay-at-home-mom years weren't nearly as rewarding in the prank department. My husband didn't appreciate the circle of cardboard I cooked into his pancakes, or the old salt-in-the-sugar-bowl switcheroo. I needed a bigger audience.

As soon as our kids got old enough, I hit them with my favorite ploy of rubber-banding the trigger on the kitchen sink sprayer so it would squirt them when they turned on the faucet.

Adding honey to the inside of the refrigerator door handle made it a double whammy. First, they got their hands all sticky, then tried to wash off the honey in the kitchen sink, where they got a face full of water.

My most successful portable stunt was the spray bottle I took to a mother-son retreat one April. During the afternoon hike, one of my sons came up behind another camper and gave a loud sneeze while I spritzed the back of the person's neck with water. (Warning: some people can get very angry.)

When I was an elementary school music teacher, my students loved the rubber vomit and rubber dog doo that I brought to school on April 1. And the remote control fart machine was always a popular item.

However, not all of my bosses appreciated receiving a chocolate cake made of toilet paper. Perhaps they would have preferred Oreos with toothpaste filling?

Along with physical gags, I also love messing with people's minds. One time I accidentally came to school wearing my shirt inside out during the last week of March. The principal heard me scold the staff for not telling me about it, so on April 1 when he noticed my shirt, he took me aside.

"Mrs. Swagerty, I think your shirt's inside out," he said.

"Yeah, I know what today is," I said. "You can't fool me."

A couple hours later I got him again when he saw me coming down the hallway from the bathroom with a streamer of toilet paper trailing out from under my skirt.

"Mrs. Swagerty," he called.

"Yes?" I answered sweetly.

"Never mind," he said, when he remembered what day it was.

But it turns out he got the last laugh.

Later that afternoon I was walking down the hall toward the office about 10 paces behind him. He opened the door and disappeared inside. A few seconds later, I followed suit. Suddenly I found myself in the men's room.

I had followed him into the bathroom instead of the office—one door's difference.

As I beat a red-faced retreat, all I could say was "April Fools." ▼

BABY SHOWERS

WHEN IT COMES to baby showers, I feel as outdated as a fan at a rock concert waving a lighter instead of a cell phone. A recent baby party showed me just how far behind the times I am.

Let's start with maternity fashions.

In my baby-bearing era, we wore clothes that were loose and floppy, voluminous cover-ups designed to hide all evidence of the baby. These garments had the grace of a two-room family tent. Perhaps it was a form of denial: if you couldn't see the bulge, it wasn't there.

Today's maternity wear is designed to highlight every inch of the expectant mom, outlining her unborn child in living, breathing spandex. You can almost see the baby kicking from across the room.

Baby accessories have changed, too. While nursing my infants, I wedged a throw pillow under my arm for support.

Now there's a special pillow, a giant circular cushion that hooks around the mother's torso like an oversized flotation device.

Airlines would do well to take note.

The baby shower I attended was a top-notch affair. Run by the mother-to-be, the aunt-to-be and their girlfriends, they went all out to make sure the dozens of attendees would have their every need met.

Lavish refreshments filled an entire corner of the room with all the major food groups represented, including a chocolate fountain gushing liquid brown.

On the invitation they gave precise instructions to their guests: "Please attach gift receipts."

This put a certain amount of pressure on a person to buy from the gift registry. The unwritten message was hard to miss: If you don't choose something good, we're taking it back.

I wasn't quite sure where to stick the gift slip, since it didn't match either the present I'd bought or the paper I wrapped it in. And if I put it in the card, it might get separated from the gift.

This was not my only dilemma.

The invitation promised a chance at winning a prize for anyone who donated a package of diapers. I'm not above bribery, so I dutifully bought a pack of diapers. That is, until I rang up the purchases and discovered the diapers cost more than the original gift. I ditched the diapers in favor of a balanced budget.

It was a good choice, since I won a prize anyway—for guessing how many nappies it took to build a three-layer diaper cake. My previous experience making a toilet paper cake must have come in handy on this game.

I didn't do as well on matching the celebrities with their babies' names, no doubt because my subscription to *People* magazine had lapsed.

After several hours of nonstop gift opening, the mother-to-be gave us our final directions, asking us to address our own thank-you note.

Why stop there? I may as well write it too, I thought. And I know what I'd say.

"Dear Lois: Thank you for the lovely gift. It was my undisputed favorite and I'd never think of taking it back."

Later I found out that the mother-to-be wasted no time exchanging the duplicate gifts. Minutes after the shower, she made a beeline to Babies "R" Us and traded them in for other items on her list.

But I didn't leave empty handed. Along with my prize, I took home a generous trail of chocolate dripped down the front of my white pants.

Note to self: Next time wear brown. ▼

MANCATION TIME

THERE'S A GREAT new word that I'm dying to use: mancation.

Man + vacation = mancation.

My husband deserves to go on one of these. When he goes away with his men's group, they're always working. They call it a retreat, but I've seen their agenda, and it takes him a week to recover when he gets back.

Guys' getaways range from the roughhewn to the luxurious, but they're a concept whose time has come.

Or maybe it's just an old idea with a new label. Perhaps my husband has been going on mancations for years, if you count his annual trip to Phoenix with 12 teammates to play baseball for a week.

Technically speaking, this trip is not for men only. The wives are invited, but few women enjoy watching the Senior Baseball World Series.

And travel conditions can be a little dicey. One year Mr. Right hitched a ride in the cab of a truck with his baseball buddy. It would have been fine if this guy hadn't also brought along a huge Doberman with a flatus problem.

One friend told me that her husband and 8-year-old son planned their own mini-mancation. Her son asked her to come camping with them, but told her she should sleep in the van and let the men sleep in the tent. That way Mom would be there to do the cooking. Hoo-boy.

Not all male vacationers want to rough it. The current craze has hotels scrambling to design weekends for men who want to be air-conditioned as well as manly. They offer chauffeured luxury cars, butlers and spa treatments. Fishing expeditions come with a gourmet chef to cook the catch of the day.

But there will always be guys who love the challenge of a week in the wild.

My girlfriend's ex-husband and adult son hiked the Grand Canyon at Christmas. I'll call them Jim and Jimmy, an intrepid father-son duo.

The way I heard it, the guys hiked up from the bottom of the canyon and camped near the top. They had lots of food lying around, which may explain what happened next.

Without warning, a flock of wild turkeys descended on their campsite, encircled the area and rapidly closed in on the men. The aggressive animals came after them, no doubt trying to prove their male dominance.

"Run for cover!" hollered the dad.

They picked up objects at hand and chucked them at the turkeys, screaming and shouting until they scared them off. The guys managed to flee the attacking herd and ran to their tents.

A little while later, Jim peeked out of his tent to see Jimmy outside about 50 yards away, surrounded again by a circle of turkeys that trapped him on the other side of the camp site.

Jimmy tried scaring them off with noise, but the angry pack only squeezed in more, hissing and squawking and jumping up at his face.

As the circle tightened, he ran out of options. Striking a karate pose and hopping on one foot, he spun around and kicked his foot toward the heads of the advancing poultry. Nearby tourists cheered him on as he escaped to safety.

Jimmy's heroics didn't go unnoticed. Not long after, a turkey activist arrived at their campsite and severely reprimanded him for attacking the turkeys.

You can bet the next time these guys plan a mancation, they'll opt for the hotel package. ▼

WHITE STRIPS

IT SOUNDED LIKE a good idea at the time. My husband and I compared our dingy smiles and agreed, "It's time to whiten our teeth."

This is a man who had professional whitening treatments by the dentist several years ago, complete with custom-made bleaching trays. I don't know why he'd want to join me in using over-the-counter products.

We found two home bleaching kits waiting in our cupboard, one 14-day kit (which had expired three years before) and one seven-day kit, so you know they were old. Current models take only three days.

Because Mr. Right was going on a trip the following week, I gave him the quicker treatment and took the longer one for myself.

That was a mistake.

On the box it claims that white strips are so easy, you can use them anytime, anywhere. But it doesn't tell you how to remember to put them on. It seems as if there's never a good time to slap the limp plastic slivers onto my teeth.

In desperation I stashed piles of the strips in various spots around the house to jog my memory. There were little stacks in my car, the back pockets of my jeans and sitting by the computer.

But I found it's hard to multitask when you're using white strips. I tried wearing them while taking a walk and talking on the phone. Somewhere during the first half mile, the plastic worked itself askew and left me with a blob of slimy bleach that I couldn't wipe on my sleeve.

Desk work seemed safer, until I licked the flap on an envelope I was mailing. One of my friends received a few bleach smears on her birthday card at no extra charge.

They say you can wear the white strips while shopping, but that could be tricky. It'd be just my luck to forget and pop in some food samples at the grocery store.

Tooth-bleaching products are constantly evolving. Every few weeks it seems there's a better, faster process with a price tag to match. Now you can choose from classic, supreme, premium plus and ultra—more varieties than you find at the gas pump, and just about as expensive.

Still, it's the time factor that makes the most difference. The classic version requires 30 minutes, twice a day, or you can wear them back to back for an hour. The speediest strips take a mere five minutes per day, but you pay extra for the convenience.

I think somebody should design tooth bleach that you could apply like Wite-Out. They had the right idea with liquid correction fluid: paint it on and blow it dry.

Speaking of innovation, let's talk a minute about flossing for the nearsighted. When is someone going to invent a flossing shield for the mirror?

I have to lean so close to see, when I'm finished my bathroom mirror looks worse than the windshield after a cross-country car trip.

Chances are, I'm not the only person who wishes for a personal house-cleaner when I'm done flossing. Meanwhile, I keep a bottle of Windex nearby.

Tooth bleaching is a lonely task. And it's not as if you get a lot of feedback for your efforts. Nobody has ever looked at me and said, "Wow, your teeth look 13 percent whiter than yesterday."

I'm now on day 25 of the 14-day kit. At this rate my teeth will be white just in time for my senior discount to kick in.

By then I'll be able to afford the three-second white strips. ▼

SAY IT IN SONG

THE PHONE RANG and I picked up to hear my husband sing, "I just called to say I love you. I just called to say how much I care."

This is not unusual. After three decades of marriage, Mr. Right and I have developed an ability to carry on entire conversations using song lyrics from bygone days.

We may be the twisted products of our musical past, but no matter what we want to say to each other, somebody has already said it better and put it to music. So why mess with perfection?

This time he was calling in from St. Louis. Before he left, he'd informed me, "I'm leaving on a jet plane, don't know when I'll be back again. Oh babe, I hate to go."

I asked what to do if I needed to get a hold of him while he was gone.

"You just call out my name, and you know wherever I am, I'll come running to see you again," he reassured me.

It's hard to come up with an original line when there are so many good lyrics. On our last vacation when he bravely wielded a plunger to unclog the toilet in our hotel room, I couldn't help breaking into song.

"Did you ever know that you're my hero? You are the wind beneath my wings."

"Aw, it's nothing," he protested. "I'm strong to the finish, 'cuz I eats me spinach." (That's from Popeye for you youngsters.)

Mr. Right is also quick with a compliment. "You are so beautiful... to me," he'll croon into my ear.

Or, "Cherish is the word I use to describe—all the feelings that I have hiding here for you inside."

Our quotations are as eclectic as they are outdated. They can jump from Billy Joel to Carole King to The Beatles in the course of a single conversation.

But the best discussions take one song and keep it going back and forth as a dialogue. He might start with James Taylor: "The secret of life is enjoying the passage of time."

"Ain't nothing to it," I agree.

Any fool can do it," he says.

Sometimes our daughter tries to communicate with us on our level, only her lyrics tend to be more original. She'll sing the tune of "You're So Vain," but change the words to "You're so lame," which gets her point across even better.

Perhaps other couples could benefit from using lyrics to convey feelings that they find difficult to express.

Take my friend Pam, for instance, whose husband is a musician in a golden oldies band. One afternoon she was slaving away in the rose garden, pruning, weeding, mulching, putting on systemic bug killer and fertilizer in the soil. Hours later she had laid 6 cubic feet of compost and 3 cubic feet of bark.

Her husband came out periodically to offer constructive criticism. Meanwhile he'd been working on the song "If I Were a Carpenter" in the garage.

Yes, indeed, thought Pam, a little miffed. If he were a carpenter, he would have actually done something to help.

Maybe he could have smoothed things over with a few well-chosen song lyrics. If he'd sung "I beg your pardon, I never promised you a rose garden," he might have gotten a little farther.

My husband knows he'd better treat me right.

Otherwise he may not like my answer when he sings, "Will you still need me, will you still feed me, when I'm 64?" ▼

IT'S ALL IN THE CARDS

IT'S TIME I got some business cards.

It seems like a no-brainer—everybody who's anybody has them. But I've never known what to call myself, hence the lack of a card.

For more than 10 years I worked as a music teacher and professional pianist, which would have been the perfect time to get an artsy-looking card with a musical logo. But it never happened.

People who asked for my card in those days chalked it up to artistic temperament when I didn't have one. They smiled indulgently when I scribbled my name and number on their show programs.

Now that I'm a writer, I'm aiming for a little flair on my business card, such as the design of a simple quill pen to inspire confidence in my writing abilities.

In November I was determined to get some cards so I asked my editor if my job was secure enough to warrant ordering business cards. He said I should probably hold off for a while. Now there's a confidence-inspiring thought.

The week before that, I'd actually gone to Kinko's to order a supply of cards.

Armed with a fistful of other people's cards for inspiration, I strode purposefully to the counter and asked for help.

Nothing prepared me for the number of decisions needed to order a business card. Heavy or light card stock? Colored or white? Smooth or textured? Single color ink or multiple? Embossed or flat? Straight edged or deckled? Monogram, logo, graphics or plain? The choices were endless.

You'd think that by having an idea already in mind, such as the image of a quill pen, it'd be easy to design a card. On the contrary, it seems that looking for a particular graphic only insures that it won't be available.

The sample binders were too heavy to lift. I slid the notebooks to one side of the counter and hunkered down to make some tough decisions.

After an hour of research, all I had to show for my efforts was a bad case of analysis paralysis. I took a few notes, jotted down some prices, and slunk home without putting in an order.

Not having a business card can either be an embarrassment or a call to greater levels of creativity. I've been known to write my contact information on anything from a used paper plate to a cone-shaped party hat. In a pinch I'll even ink my information onto someone's hand.

A friend once confided to me, "Writing your name and e-mail address on a napkin is slightly less than professional."

I'm not disputing the fact.

When I attended my first writer's conference last year, the conference guidelines encouraged all the writers to bring plenty of business cards.

Somehow it slipped my mind in the final weeks before the gathering, and I ended up empty-handed in the midst of a feeding frenzy of writers and agents.

I can only imagine all the book deals that passed me by for lack of having a business card. Not to mention the lack of having a book.

As soon as I get my business cards, I'll feel like a real writer.

As the song says, "If you get an outfit you can be a cowboy, too."

What's that you say?

I need a website? ▼

THE MOTHER OF INVENTION

MY MOTHER DIED in 1980. I think she would have loved some of the products invented since then, and not only the high-tech devices. I'm talking about everyday items, such as Zip-lock bags, that would have thrilled her no end.

Mom came from the old school of plastic bag savers; she washed them out and hung them on the line to dry. She could have had a ball with Zip-locks. They stand up by themselves and can even march in rows across the counter.

Like an Inspector Gadget of the kitchen, my mom was an efficiency expert, the queen of labor-saving devices. I grew up thinking that every household was equipped with tomato knives and mushroom brushes, meat grinders and corn-on-the-cob buttering doodads.

She always appreciated innovation.

When Velcro came out in the 1960s—a by-product of the space program, along with Tang orange drink—she was the first one on our block to use it for sewing.

Once she made me a school dress that featured a foot-long strip of Velcro up the front. It made the bosom stick out stiffly at an angle when I sat down, so I was forever pushing it back in.

"Aw, Mom," I complained. "Do I have to wear this?"

While other sixth-grade girls were stuffing socks in their bras, I was pounding at my chest to keep it flat.

Stain sticks would have rocked my mother's world. She used a scrub brush with gray and gritty Lava soap on stains. Imagine if she could have rubbed some goo on a spot and let it disappear in the washing machine.

I can only guess how she would react at the sight of me pulling a tube of Tide to Go out of my purse and erasing the smear from a strawberry I just dropped on my white shirt.

Post-it notes? I'm not sure exactly when they came along, but I know she'd adore them.

The original concept came out in the form of large, adhesive sheets you could tack up on the wall like a bulletin board. I used to throw things against mine at the office to see what would stick, sort of like flinging cooked spaghetti noodles at the refrigerator door.

From there it was just a short, inspired leap to the colorful sticky notes we use today. And did you realize they were an accident? Some sort of failure by the glue inventors. You know some heads had to roll on that one.

Speaking of adhesives, let's not overlook the clear, snot-like material often found on junk mail. It's that line of stretchy glue that comes on slick-paper mailings. Hard to believe somebody's making a killing from inventing rubber boogers, but it's true.

They are loads of fun to peel up and roll between your fingers. I personally enjoy hanging them from my nose—but not in public.

Which reminds me: When I was a kid, we would suck on a piece of Scotch tape until the glue separated from the cellophane. I'm probably not the only one who did this, or who spread Elmer's glue on my palms just so I could peel it off when it dried. But for the record, I wasn't a paste eater.

If my mom were around today, I bet she'd be one of those cool grannies who listens to an iPod and talks with her grandkids online.

She'd definitely have a cell phone, and if I called to wish her a happy Mother's Day, odds are I'd end up on call waiting.

I'd sure love the chance to find out. ▼

ROLL THE CREDITS

I LOVE GOING to the movies even more than I love going through the car wash, and that's saying a lot.

The car wash experience features so many thrills, it's hard to know where to begin.

It's satisfying from the moment you're propelled with a lurch onto the conveyor belt, to the spinning tri-colored soapsuds, to the rubber hula skirt that dances over your windshield, to the soothing mist at the end. And it finishes with the roar of a wind tunnel that deposits you gleaming and spotless out the other end. It feels almost like being born, only a lot quicker.

So how can going to the movies compare with that?

For one thing, movies last a whole lot longer, but they can be just as satisfying.

On our first date in 1972, my future husband and I went to see *Fiddler on the Roof* in Hollywood. We were running late, sprinting from the parking lot to reach the movie as it was starting. (No 15-minute previews in those days.)

"I'm sorry that we're missing the beginning," said Mr. Right.

"That's okay," I said. "I've already seen this movie with my boyfriend."

Maybe it wasn't the greatest way to start a new relationship, but 35 years later we're still going to the movies together.

A few compatibility issues have cropped up, such as how far back to sit in the theater and how much violence I can tolerate. I don't even bother taking him to subtitled films. Last week I felt bad for a man sitting through a chick flick. His snores were louder than the sound track.

But when we see a complicated movie, my husband's a great person to have on hand. He can explain anything that I don't understand.

Something about his face must inspire confidence in other moviegoers, too. After one movie with an intricate plot, a woman came up and asked him to explain the movie to her. I guess he has a knowing look. Either that, or she was desperate.

I know about desperation. Once I went to see "Lord of the Rings" by myself and couldn't make it through the whole thing without a bathroom break. I tapped the women in front of me on the shoulder and asked her if she'd tell me what I missed when I got back. She turned around, squinted at me in the dim light from the screen and said, "Mrs. Swagerty, is that you?"

It turned out she was a mom from a school where I'd taught the previous year. So technically, I wasn't accosting a complete stranger.

One of the best parts of a movie is the credits. In fact, I keep a list of interesting roles collected from the closing credits. One of my favorites is the Large Thuggish Man.

Can you picture this fellow calling up his sweet, old mother?

"Guess what, Mom. I finally got my big break in the movies!"

"That's wonderful, dear. What part are you playing?"

"The Large Thuggish Man."

"Oh Sonny, I always knew you'd go far."

Other roles on my list include the Scary Looking Man, Flighty Girl, Smug Intern, Snaggle-toothed Monk, and a whole cast of characters on busses—the Large Man on Bus, Another Man on Bus and Irritated Man on Bus.

As the saying goes, "There are no small parts, only small actors."

I think it's time I auditioned for my own part: Woman Going Through Car Wash. ▼

IRONY: THE OPPOSITE OF WRINKLY

THE WAY I figure it, if one out of three of my kids learned to iron, I did a decent job of parenting.

After all, in baseball a batting average of .333 is remarkable.

Ironing is one of those skills—along with mending and gardening—that didn't get modeled much when my kids were growing up. Nobody said I had to be good at everything.

Thanks to permanent press fabrics and poor eyesight, the clothes always looked decent to me. If I timed the dryer cycle just right, I could snatch my husband's dress shirts out while they tumbled. It was my little game to catch them before the wrinkles had a chance to bake in.

As for mending, I just waited until the kids outgrew the ripped clothes and gave them away—the clothes, not the kids.

Although I didn't iron often, I did invest in a top-of-the-line model of iron. Once the nonstick coating began to flake off my old college iron, I thought I'd go for the gold and buy a Rowenta.

Simply owning such a classy iron made me feel special, and on the rare occasions when I actually used it, it glided along like a hot knife through butter.

My mom used the same theory when she bought me a good sewing machine for my college graduation. Knowing that the sewing gene had skipped a generation, she didn't begrudge it to me. Instead, she insisted that I be well equipped in case a fit of mending overtook me at a later date.

The last time I went to the local hardware store to buy a new ironing board cover, I was stunned at the selection.

- Light use—for those who iron at least once a month
- Moderate use—for those who iron at least twice a month
- Frequent use—for those who iron at least once a week
- Heavy use—for those who iron at least twice a week.

Not finding a product for someone who irons less than once a month, I left the store empty handed.

Earlier this year, blogger Lisa Hunter joked that ironing is replacing cooking as an upscale hobby in New York.

Paris has a reality TV show called the Golden Iron, in which contestants compete at ironing dress shirts. The winning time in the October 2006 meet was a sizzling 4 minutes 29 seconds.

And for anyone who's bored stiff with ironing in their own homes, there's the Extreme Ironing Bureau, which has transformed ironing into an international sport.

The bureau defines extreme ironing as "the latest danger sport that combines the thrills of an extreme outdoor activity with the satisfaction of a well-pressed shirt."

"To do extreme ironing, you must carry an iron, ironing board, and laundry as you participate in some other 'extreme' activity. The idea is to do some ironing (and, preferably, get someone to photograph you in the act) while rock climbing, snowboarding, skydiving, surfing, cattle-roping, scuba diving or what-have-you," says writer Joe Kissell.

The coveted Rowenta trophy goes to the contender with the fastest speed, the fewest wrinkles and the least number of injuries.

Thanks, but I can burn myself standing still.

It seems that those who master the fine art of ironing can go far.

I'll be watching to see if any of my kids end up taking it to the extreme—which, for me, means ironing more than once a month. ▼

THE LIGHTER SIDE OF SIDE EFFECTS

I'VE BECOME AN expert on medication side effects in the past year.

For example, I'm taking one drug that can cause constipation *and* diarrhea. You'd think the two would cancel each other out. No such luck.

Then there's the pill that can impair your thinking. But how would you know? Trust me, it doesn't help to ask your kids.

You're supposed to carry a card that lists all the medications you're taking. I think my husband should carry a card that says, "I don't beat her—she's taking blood thinners."

Lists of drug side effects are so long that you tend to stop reading. You know the drug company is trying to cover its backside when the list goes on longer than the Jones section of the White Pages.

I feel bad for the pharmaceutical companies—well, as bad as you can feel for a multi-billion-dollar industry that's raking in the revenue.

They are stuck with whatever the test respondents put down on their survey, no matter how far-fetched. If there's a guy who gets a toothache after trying hemorrhoid cream, it has to show up on the list of possible side effects.

My husband and I got an inside glimpse into the pharmaceutical world when we lunched with a friend who is a research doctor for one of the big drug companies. He said they'd poured millions into inventing a miracle drug that would raise your good cholesterol, only to find out that it had one disturbing side effect: it shortened your life expectancy.

Even scarier are those discreet TV commercials that mention possible sexual side effects. They don't say exactly what problem you might have, so it leaves you guessing, which can almost be worse than knowing.

Then there's the domino effect.

That's when a medication causes a chain reaction that just keeps on going. For instance, when a statin drug lowered my cholesterol, it also reduced my hormone levels, which triggered insomnia, hot flashes and chronic weepiness.

Nowhere on the drug sheet did it warn my family that I'd become such an embarrassment. You can see why drug companies wouldn't want to take responsibility for the entire chain of events, but personally, I'd have appreciated a little more truth in advertising.

The best thing I ever learned about a side effect came from a college friend named Ken.

We'd just finished Thanksgiving dinner at our house when he bolted from the table into the living room. I followed him and watched as he lay down stiffly on his left side on our green shag carpet.

"What are you doing?" I asked.

"Just wait," he said. "Did you know that lying on your left side makes you pass gas?"

I beat a hasty retreat from the room, but filed away the tidbit for future reference.

Evidently my chiropractor didn't know this factoid, because he put me on my left side to adjust my spine today. The result was predictable.

Natural remedies can have side effects, too. After taking my daily Omega-3s, I've noticed that I spend the next two hours burping up fish oil. They say it helps to put the capsules in the freezer, which I guess is supposed to fool your stomach into thinking you're having ice cream.

But you never see a warning on the fish oil bottle. For all I know, I could start sprouting scales after three months on the stuff. I'll keep you posted. ▼

PART FIVE

Summer Again

THE WAR OF THE ROSES

I AM LOSING the war against aphids.

After waging the Battle of the Bugs for many years, I'm ready to give up and let them have the rose garden.

They might as well take over the lease. Let them sign on the dotted line and it's a done deal. Call it squatters' rights—they can have all the roses they have wrecked. They can share ownership with the little black bugs living on the underside of the leaves.

The only thing green about my thumb is the aphids that were crawling on it after I touched a rose bud the other day.

At first I thought it was a nicely textured green bud. But then I saw it was carpeted wall-to-wall with aphids.

These must have been teen aphids. Evidently I caught them playing a game of How Many Can We Crowd Onto a Rose Bud. Some of us remember a similar pastime of packing people into a Volkswagen bug when we were young.

A non-gardener like me has no business trying to grow roses. They have more diseases, pests, and blights than Madonna has bustiers.

Searching for weapons in my garden shed, I found an arsenal of sprays and powders with scary pictures on them. Pictures of black spot, powdery mildew and rust. Pictures of aphids, thripes and bristly rose slugs. And warnings on all the products that featured skull-and-crossbones.

There has to be a natural way to get rid of these pests, I thought. I don't want to get this toxic stuff on me.

I got on the Internet and searched for natural aphid cures. Up popped recipes for onion, garlic and hot pepper sprays. Ads for organic soaps horticultural oils. Strategies for importing ladybugs as natural predators.

One remedy suggested putting sheets of aluminum foil around the base of the plants to confuse the aphids with reflected sunlight. This might work if we weren't stuck between the months of May Gray and June Gloom.

It seems that aphids are attracted to yellow. One site recommended setting out large, yellow containers of water to drown them. Another claimed that you should drape banana skins over the branches. In a day or less the aphids are supposed to be gone. I tried this one. It added a festive, trashy look to the garden but didn't disturb the aphids one bit.

Didn't I read somewhere that spraying soap on the rose bushes would do the trick? When I checked my house for soaps, all I could find were detergents, which we know will cause dishpan hands. But would it prove fatal to aphids?

Suddenly I remembered the movie "My Big Fat Greek Wedding" with its many uses for Windex. I was about to grab my Windex bottle and head for the roses when I saw another option.

One website said to crush some aphids between your thumb and forefinger, squeezing them as they feed on leaves and stems. If you drop their bodies on the ground around the rose bushes, the carcasses put out a scent that acts as a deterrent.

This approach appealed to my get-it-done mentality. No waiting around for the long-term systemic approach; I was looking for quick results. So I got out my hose, blasted the bushes, and left a few carefully placed bodies as a warning to the other aphids.

Our backyard now hosts fewer aphids and a few more roses.

I also acquired a Green Thumb—at least that's the name printed on the side of my new watering can. ▼

NAME GAMES

I'VE ALWAYS BEEN plagued by androgynous names—those tricky appellations that make you stop and wonder about the gender of the owner.

It seems as if every group I've ever joined has had one couple whose names stump me. For example, I once was part of a group that included Jerry and Mickey. They were the cutest couple and we loved them dearly. But when conversing with one of them, I always had to stop and ponder which name to use.

After struggling for two years, I finally went to the group leader and confessed my problem.

"It's easy to remember," he said. "Mickey is the boy, just like Mickey Mouse."

After that it was no sweat. I just pictured him with big black ears.

In December, when I ran into this couple again after an absence of five years, I greeted him with confidence. "Hi, Mickey Mm..." barely stopping myself in time.

Another group had Rudi and Randy, and Kendall and Derek. You can bet that I used "Hey you" a lot when addressing these folks.

It's doubly perplexing when a name that you grew up thinking was for guys switches over to gals. That's what happened with Kendall, which was my friend's brother's name when I was young. Now we've got a little girl next door with the same name.

Sometimes it's a cultural thing as in the south, where girls often carry a family last name as their first name. Such is the case with our southern buddies Bradford and Stephen. Once you figure out the wife's family name, you're okay.

Other people tend to go for long strings of names. We like to call people by their initials—RJ, TJ or AJ—but in some cases they choose an entire acronym. Our Alabama friends Fletcher and Barber (I'll let you guess which is which) gave their son four names, William Elliot Barber Bancroft, and called him WEBB for short.

Parents are getting a lot more creative in naming their kids. And there's a lovely international flavor to the names as the population becomes more diverse.

My dance teacher friend sent me some interesting names from one of the local elementary schools: Zyra, Andokar, Feloza, Zoyah, Shendo, Shadi, Pixie and VyVy. And these are just the first names.

On the other hand, there's still the gender question which you really need to get right when you're a school teacher. It's one thing to accidentally call my friend Brian Janey by his last name instead of his first. He's old enough to laugh it off. But it's a whole different matter in an elementary school.

One time I was substitute teaching and used the wrong pronoun to refer to a student. The student was a he and I thought he was a she. Now that's a mistake that's hard to recover from, and even harder for the poor student.

Afterwards I always kept a seating chart with names and a note if there was any doubt. For every boy Jordan there was also a girl Jordan, and a girl Taylor for every boy Taylor, so I developed my own little gender notation.

It's especially difficult for school teachers to name their own children. No matter what name they choose, a child with the same name comes along in their classroom and makes an indelible mark for better or worse.

But it must be even harder if you're a meteorologist.

I heard there's recently been a sharp decline in girls named Katrina. ▼

DRIVING YOU BANANAS

BUYING FRUIT IS a complex art.

It's so complicated that I'm thinking of going back to school to take classes in fruit selection.

After watching shoppers in various venues—from the grocery store to the farmers market to the warehouse store—I realize that my education is sorely lacking.

I've gotten by so far on urban myths and tips handed down from previous generations, but I never know if they're fact or fiction.

When it comes to choosing melons, there are the smellers, the slappers and the thumpers—three distinct schools of thought.

Me? I was raised as a watermelon thumper.

I think there ought to be some rules about picking bananas.

Last week in Trader Joe's I saw a shopper who systematically went through each banana bunch on the display and tore off the best one or two to keep for herself. She collected a bag of pristine singles and doubles, ranging in ripeness from green to yellow, and left her discards for the rest of us.

That's just wrong. I hope they caught her on the surveillance camera and sent her a citation in the mail.

This morning I stood in the fruit section of Costco for 10 minutes trying to select a pineapple. People came and people went, and many shared helpful advice along the way.

First, there were the sniffers. One man smelled at least a dozen pineapples in a row, tossing them aside left and right to expose the next layer of boxes. He told me they had to smell sweet on the outside to be sweet on the inside.

Then there were the leaf-pullers. Supposedly if you can pull a leaf out of the top easily, the fruit is ripe, which also explains the pile of loose foliage on the floor.

Bottom-checkers lift up the fruit and check underneath to see if it is mold-free and yields to a gentle pressure.

Eyeballers go by the color. If it's golden, then it's ready to cut. And according to the TV chef at the local market, you should look for eyes that are plump and shiny. Who knew pineapples had eyes in the first place?

While I'm on the subject, who decided to install TVs in the produce section of the supermarket? It's the last place in the world where I want to watch TV. I spend more energy wishing I could turn it off than I do shopping.

But back to pineapples.

I lingered so long by the pineapple bin that I finally got the scoop of a lifetime. One lady lowered her voice and gave me a hint as valuable as an insider's racing tip.

"You should look for eyes that are uniform in size," she confided. "A man who works at the Dole plant in Hawaii told me this."

I'd never noticed that pineapple eyes could vary, but sure enough—some were equal and others had bigger eyes at the bottom and squinchy ones at the top. Some looked as if the pineapple had run out of room and had to squeeze in the last few rows, similar to when I write on poster board.

This woman seemed trustworthy, so I went with her method, carefully measuring the pineapple eyes between my thumb and forefinger.

Oddly enough, after giving away all that free advice, nobody was willing to risk picking out a pineapple for me.

"Good luck," was the parting comment of each.

No matter which piece of fruit I choose, it never fails: I always wish I had the one in the other person's basket. ▼

CREATING CREATIVITY

"HOW DO YOU come up with ideas for your columns?" folks ask me.

Lots of people suggest topics they think I should write about. Usually I smile and agree that their ideas would make a fabulous article.

Secretly I think, "Why don't *you* write about that?"

Then there are others who wonder about my sanity. "You're a little quirky, aren't you?" commented one reader.

Maybe I'm quirky, but I prefer the word interesting. When my most off-beat friend once told someone that I was her quirkiest friend, I got a little scared.

Sometimes I surprise my own husband. "Did you really do this?" he asked when he read about me hanging rubber adhesive from my nose.

Keep in mind I was mostly around kids for many years.

How-to books on fostering creativity abound. Some suggest standing on your head, chewing herbs or traveling to exotic locales.

But my formula is simple: Do something boring. I can always count on activities such as taking a shower, drying my hair or taking a walk to unleash the creative juices.

There's something magical about mindless repetition that unlocks the floodgates of the brain.

Perhaps that's why swinging is so good for children. When my kids were little, all the developmental books recommended swinging. The rhythmic back-and-forth motion was supposed to make them smarter than the average bear.

For me, performing repetitive tasks frees up the creative side of the brain—I can never remember whether it's the right or left side—

to spew out ideas. Sometimes they come out in such a rush, it's impossible to halt their flow.

I first stumbled upon this discovery back in the days when I regularly vacuumed the house. After cleaning the carpet in one or two rooms, it generated such a long list of ideas to try, things to do and people to call, that I never got back to vacuuming again—an added bonus.

Then I noticed another phenomenon. Every time I took a shower, inspiration flowed faster than the water from the faucet. Since I couldn't trust my memory, I would scribble notes in the steam on the glass door.

The same thing happened when drying my hair. Take a monotonous process, combine it with warmth and a droning noise, and *voila!* You have a recipe for instant creativity.

After dashing, dripping through the house every few minutes to write down my ideas, it got to the point where I had to allow an extra half hour for getting ready.

Nowadays I've stashed paper and pen in most of my creative zones, but I believe the real solution is still waiting to be invented.

They could make a combination hair dryer/laptop computer that you could drop in the sink without electrocuting yourself.

Or a fog-free message board for inside the shower. You could hang the multicolored markers right next to your soap-on-a-rope.

How about a kneeling pad with a microphone to capture those revelations that sneak up on you while you're gardening?

I've decided I need to get a miniature recorder to hang around my neck when I'm out on a walk. It's got to be easier than calling home on my cell phone to leave messages for myself.

It's time to write another column, but my shower is over and my hair is dried. I guess I'll have to wait until tomorrow for the next brainstorm.

Either that, or break out the vacuum cleaner. ▼

TROUBLE WITH TRAVEL

I DON'T TRAVEL often. But when I do, I do it inefficiently. I pack too late, take too much, and forget to refill all my little containers of lotions and gels.

Usually it takes an extra suitcase just for my pillows. There's a neck pillow, a between-the-knees pillow, a back roll and an elbow Sqush—an entire pillow family that travels with me.

And the snacks. The way I pack food, you'd think the airport hallways weren't lined with wall-to-wall eateries. For fear of running out of provisions, I stuff my carry-on bag with all the major food groups.

I also bring along three different flavors of Airborne vitamin formula: daytime, nighttime and chewables.

People behind me love it when I hold up the line as we're boarding to ask for water and a cup to dissolve my Airborne.

Then there are the books. Choosing the right book to take on the plane is a dilemma. You can't rely on the good one you've almost finished because it will run out mid-flight and leave you stranded. And it's always risky to start a new one because you might hate it after the first few pages. (This is why smart people own e-readers.) But no matter which book I bring, I always see one in the airport bookstore that I want more.

There are people who are travel experts, but I'm not one of them.

They have 20 color-coordinated outfits derived from only four garments made from wrinkle-free fabrics. Their baggage matches and the zippers all work. They fit two weeks of clothes into one Zip-lock and suck out the air with a vacuum hose.

Savvy travelers check the Internet for the weather forecast at their destination and take only the appropriate clothing. I read the forecast and add a few more outfits just in case.

The way I see it, if I don't travel often enough to become good at it, why should I feel bad?

On the other hand, it doesn't take much to thrill me. On a recent flight, a miniature box of Sun-maid raisins made my day. That—plus sitting in the exit row with extra leg room and having an empty seat beside for elbow room. Top it off with easy access to the nearest lavatory and you've got one happy traveler.

My travel habits can be annoying, it's true. Perhaps this is where I should confess that I tore out a page from the *Delta-Sky* magazine on my last flight.

For the record, it was not my idea. When I asked Mr. Right to help me remember the name of a restaurant I wanted to try that was featured in the magazine, he said, "Rip it out."

So I did. No sirens went off and no arrest was made.

It's always fun to skim the latest issue of *Skymall* to check out the basic necessities of life. The pop-up hot dog and bun toaster is a favorite, although I wonder if the kind of people who could afford it would be the type to eat a hot dog.

Speaking of pork, a recent trip took us to Memphis, where we found out why it's nicknamed Fat City. All they serve in the entire town is pork ribs, the biggest decision being whether to eat them wet or dry.

It does no good to order something besides pork barbeque in Memphis. It's like ordering something besides the food that a restaurant is named for—a cardinal rule that I never follow and my husband never breaks.

Until yesterday, when he made the mistake of ordering steak at a restaurant called the Bread Basket.

You'd think he was a novice traveler like me. ▼

COMPLIMENT JEOPARDY

I'VE NEVER BEEN good at returning compliments.

For example, my husband said to me, "Your hair looks good."

"Thanks," I said, and went back to working on the laptop.

Next time I looked up, he was craning his neck all around in a vain effort to get me to comment on his own hair. It was then that I realized the extent of my reciprocal compliment deficiency.

I always thought it was unoriginal to return a compliment right after you've received one. I mean, how transparent is it when somebody says, "I like your shirt" to turn around and remark about their clothes? But I'm afraid society expects it.

Or as Mr. Right claims, "Originality is highly overrated."

Complimenting others' appearance seems like a basic social skill; still I seldom remember to do it spontaneously. I need a mental nudge to get me started.

Sometimes I make a special point to give the first word of praise. Then I'm off the hook; the other person has to worry about being a copycat—assuming that anybody else gives it a second thought.

This works well until it triggers a volley of flattering remarks that makes your neck swivel back and forth like a spectator at Wimbledon.

Another technique I've tried is to vary the categories, like a game of "Jeopardy."

You walk into the office and somebody says, "Nice jacket." This opens the category of Clothes for $100, so you can either go to Clothes for $200—"Where'd you get those shoes?" or switch to Hair for $100 and sing out, "Cute hairdo."

After clothes and hair, you can try something different, such as Weight for $100: "Have you lost weight?" Or if a person has just returned from vacation, you can comment on their general appearance: "You look tan/rested/wonderful" or any combination thereof.

If you want to score a Daily Double, combine two of the above categories and you'll hit it out of the ballpark. (Yes, I realize I'm mixing my game metaphors.)

But I caution you: Only in a compliment emergency should you bring up the subject of surgeries: "Nice face lift" and "Great breast job" are comments to avoid at all cost. If you accidentally let it slip, follow up with a quick, "Did I really say that out loud?" and move on to something safer, such as the weather.

After all, where would we be without small talk? It's possible that offices everywhere would grind to a halt without the lubricating effect of chitchat.

Perhaps it's the most civilized way of easing into the day. Nobody wants to have a heavy-duty conversation first thing in the morning. In fact, just to be safe, my kids have warned me never to say anything to them before noon.

And why do they call it "paying" a compliment? If I don't pay up, does that mean I owe you a compliment? In that case you can just bill me when I forget.

It'd be a lot easier to take care of compliments with my charge card. Put it on my bill and automatically send out admiring remarks on a timely basis. That way I can get airline miles while I'm at it.

I think there's a niche market for people like me who could use a little help. How about a website for delivering e-compliments? Vary the date and the topic, and you've got it made with one click of the mouse.

It seems that no compliment is too flimsy or too repetitive.

The only bad compliment is an insincere one—or one delivered too early in the morning. ▼

HIKING MUST-HAVES

WE WEREN'T PLANNING on going hiking.

There we were, vacationing in Idyllwild, California, my husband and I. Soaring San Jacinto mountains beckoned, tempting us with their rocky peaks. But we had come unprepared for a serious hike.

Why let the lack of equipment stop us? We decided to go.

Our first hurdle was filling out the National Park Service permit, which required us to carry a trowel if we wanted to use the trails. Waste must be buried at least eight inches deep, it specified.

We searched every drawer and cupboard of our rented cottage. The only trowel-shaped object we could find was a soup spoon, so we packed it just in case.

On the morning of the big hike, we dressed in shorts, T-shirts, tennies and straw gardening hats, with an extra ration of toilet paper stuffed in my pocket. My husband's black socks added special appeal to his outfit.

We unloaded my backpack purse and filled it with water, sunscreen, bandages and snacks—and the spoon. Mr. Right looped the spindly black straps over his shoulders.

As we pulled into a parking space at the national park, we saw another couple getting ready to hike. They were decked out in full hiking regalia. Heavy boots, nylon shin guards, padded backpacks, absorbent bandanas and foldable aluminum walking sticks.

Next to them we looked like the Beverly Hillbillies.

We started first and plodded our way slowly up the first slope. In a few minutes the other couple overtook us and we politely stood aside to let them pass. They didn't say anything about our equipment, but I could see them eyeing my husband's socks.

Five minutes later, we caught up with them as they stopped to peel off their shirts and chug down bottles of Gatorade. We crept by in our snaillike pace.

"Just like the tortoise and the hare," said my husband.

We stopped often to rest and enjoy the view. Two hours and 2-1/2 miles later, we reached our goal, Saddle Junction, and then cruised a half-mile more to Skunk Cabbage Meadow.

After a brief snack, we started down the mountain. Mr. Right estimated that with gravity on our side, we'd make it back in only half the time it took us to climb up. Since he was on the math team in high school, I didn't question his theory. . .out loud.

By this time the sun was beating down and the day was heating up.

"Doesn't this heat feel good?" he said. "It's dry heat." Dry heat always sounds like dry heaves to me.

I turned into a shade-seeking missile, dodging from patch to patch. Every time I reached cover, I stopped to enjoy it.

"That's bad shade," said my husband at one stop.

There's no such thing as bad shade, I thought.

He pointed down the trail 50 yards ahead, and when we got there he said, "Feel how much cooler this shade is?"

We whiled away the miles by belting out theme songs from old TV shows. "Hawaii Five-O" was my favorite with its compelling lyrics of "Dunt-dunt-dunt-dunt dun dun, dunt-dunt-dunt dunt DUN." Friendly hikers joined in with the words to "Gilligan's Island."

It turned out to be a pleasant hike. And if you asked me why we went, I'd have to say it was just for the hill of it.

On our way back, a lady passed us carrying a dog in her backpack.

I sure hope that doggie brought a trowel. ▼

THE FIVE-SECOND RULE

IT'S TRUE THAT honesty is the best policy. But it's also true that what you don't know won't hurt you.

What's a person to do when these two laws collide?

Company was coming for dinner. I'd cooked all day for the occasion and made a huge pasta salad.

About five minutes before the guests were to arrive, I dropped the entire bowl of salad upside down on the floor.

Since it was too late to replace the salad, I quickly scooped up the part that hadn't touched the floor and popped it back into the bowl. Scraping up the rest with a spatula, I rinsed it in hot water, reintroduced it to the salad and sloshed on more salad dressing to make it blend in.

The hardest part was getting the spilled dressing off the floor. I wiped and wiped, but when Son Two came into the kitchen to taste the salad, he slipped on the grease spot.

"What'd you spill?" he asked. "I just washed this floor." That was true—he'd helped me clean the kitchen floor the day before.

"I'm not telling," I said.

As soon as he walked away, I worked on the oil slick some more. It finally came clean, but only after using Windex. I crossed my fingers and hoped the dinner guests wouldn't smell the ammonia when they walked in the door.

All went well. The dinner was a hit and I kept mum about my little mishap.

Later that night after the guests were gone, I could hold in the truth no longer. I confessed all to my two sons.

Son Two had a look of admiration in his eyes. I could see that I'd gone up a few notches in his estimation.

Son One was stunned. He wore a hurt look on his face that said, "You betrayed me, Mom." He claimed he'd found a hair in his salad.

I felt bad. He was probably reliving his whole life, trying to figure out other times when I'd served him dinner off the floor. I wondered if I should've kept quiet after all.

The next day I read an article that eased my tortured mind. A recent study by a group of scientific researchers in Connecticut reported that the five-second rule is inaccurate.

You know—the rule that says if you pick up food within five seconds of dropping it on the ground, it won't hurt you to eat it.

A college professor and her students have challenged the prevailing wisdom of the so-called five-second rule, which for generations has governed how long dropped food can remain on floors uncontaminated.

The safety zone, they found, is really 30 seconds.

A previous study from 2003 had confirmed the five-second rule, but it used a floor smeared with E. coli virus, which was overkill, if you ask me. The current researchers wanted to use a more realistic scenario.

After dropping moist apple slices and dry Skittles onto a busy cafeteria floor and testing the bacteria levels, their study concluded that "instead of a five-second rule for moist foods that have fallen, the standard should be 30 seconds."

Germaphobes everywhere breathed a sigh of relief.

Although I'd never claim you could eat off my floors, my kitchen was probably a lot cleaner than the college cafeteria, and I'm sure I scooped up the pasta within 30 seconds. Next time I'll get out the stop watch.

As for my moral dilemma, the jury's still out. But I have to admit: confession is good for the soul. ▼

SIZE MATTERS

LAST WEEK I bought some cherries that were so big, they were almost the size of plums.

When I mentioned this to Favorite Dotter, she wasn't convinced. "Yeah, right," she scoffed.

The next day our neighbors gave us a bag of homegrown plums from their backyard. I pulled out the smallest plum and held it next to the largest cherry to illustrate my point. She was still unimpressed.

I may have exaggerated a bit, but oversized fruit still amazes me. We have some naval oranges on our tree that ought to be tested for steroids. And I've got blueberries in the fridge right now that could be used for the shot put.

It's easy to get carried away when estimating size. Just ask any fisherman.

When my mom was diagnosed with a tumor in the 1970s, our friend Bill got on the phone to send the word out. He started telling people it was as big as a baseball.

By the end of the calls, like in the game of Telephone, it had morphed into a fruit and grown to the size of a cantaloupe. Morbid humor, but there you have it.

On the other end of the spectrum, there are the minifruits.

I bought a watermelon the other day that was as small as a grapefruit. We didn't really need it, but it was so cute, I couldn't resist. And it fit easily into the refrigerator after it was cut, a distinct advantage.

Immediately I emailed Son One in L.A. to tell him that I'd found the perfect watermelon-for-one. You can imagine how much he loves hearing from me.

Miniatures of anything have a special appeal. I love the tiny containers that you find in the travel-size bins at the drug store. Like a squirrel stockpiling nuts for the winter, I keep my own little stash.

The last time I got sucked into the travel aisle, I came home with a bagful of shampoos, creams, pastes and lotions. When I gave the undersized can of shaving cream to my husband, he said, "You already got me three of these."

So sue me.

Son Two saw the collection and commented, "What'd you do, Mom—rob the prize basket at the dentist?"

The secret is out. I only go to the dentist because I like all the items in her grownup prize basket. I return every six months just for the office supplies. Don't try to convince me it's cheaper to buy my own glue sticks and miniature markers than to pay for a dental cleaning and X-rays.

Things are always cuter when they're smaller. Look at all the people who have puppies and kittens—or babies. The regrets may come when they grow bigger, but you can't beat the appeal of something small.

For a while some girlfriends of mine had a contest to see who could carry the smallest purse. My friend Liz won hands down with her credit-card-sized handbag and a cell phone no bigger than a Fig Newton. I couldn't even compete.

When it comes to cars, she'd always dreamed of driving a Miata. Nowadays she hankers after the Mini Cooper.

My desires are much simpler.

There's an adorable little can of Static Guard in my daughter's room that I've had my eye on for a while.

I'm planning on borrowing it as soon as she leaves on her next trip. ▼

DIRTY WORK

"GOT POOP? WE Scoop!" said the ad in the coupon clipper magazine. So claims a local pet waste cleanup service.

But what really caught my eye was the company's slogan printed below in tiny letters: "Leave the Disgusting Job to Us."

They want revolting chores?

How about cleaning up vomit? That's a service I would have paid plenty for in my early years of parenting.

It stands to reason that if there's someone in Cortez, Colorado who can suck prairie dogs out of the ground, there has to be a way to vacuum up vomit. I bet they could back a truck into your driveway and unfurl the hoses. Just call 1-800-Upchuck.

I'm the kind of person who gags when I smell the contents of someone else's stomach, so when our kids were young, I let my husband handle the cleanup whenever heaving was involved.

"Sorry, I'm allergic to vomit," I'd say, and handing him the extra-large rubber gloves, I'd excuse myself from the scene of the grime.

Family vomiting stories—along with camping stories—are the stuff of legends. There's the time my husband and I went out to dinner and left Son One in charge of the two younger kids. He must have been about 13 at the time.

When we returned, we discovered that our daughter had gotten sick. She tried to hit the trash can by her bedside, but instead had hurled her dinner into the computer printer conveniently located on the nightstand.

Thankfully, our son cleaned it up before we got home. I was so happy it hadn't happened on my watch that I paid him triple overtime for babysitting.

Documents printed after that night always smelled a little funny to me.

On another occasion, Son Two ate spaghetti for dinner and washed it down with a red beverage. When he erupted with the flu later that night, he sprayed the carpet and walls all the way down the hall from his bedroom to the bathroom. It looked like a crime scene. All that was missing was the yellow tape and the chalk outline of a body.

Vomiting scenes in movies simultaneously attract and repel. In my opinion, the classic barf-o-rama during the pie eating contest in *Stand By Me* is worth the entire price of the movie rental.

Why is someone else's mess so much worse to clean up than your own?

And what is it about hair in the drain? Hair isn't disgusting on your head. It only becomes repulsive in the sink or when it clogs up the drain.

My husband finds a strange satisfaction in digging hair out of the shower drain. Maybe it's because we happen to have the perfect tools—a pair of foot-long forceps and some 10-inch tweezers leftover from my job at a surgical instrument company in Philadelphia.

He gets out the operating instruments and pops off the drain cover. Minutes later he extracts what looks like a small rodent and holds it up victoriously. I run when he tries to show it to me.

I've heard there's a TV show with people doing dirty jobs. Teenagers doing dirty work? That's not a reality show, that's a fantasy.

You have to wonder where it will all end. And how far the pet cleanup company will go to find disgusting tasks.

Personally, I'm happy to leave the dirty work to somebody else. Instead of tossing my cookies, I'd rather be baking them.

What's that 800-number again? ▼

FASHION FAUX PAS

I'M WRITING A sequel to Nora Ephron's bestselling book, *I Feel Bad about My Neck*.

The title: *I Feel Bad about My Clothes.*

When it comes to shopping for styles, mixing and matching or picking outfits, I'm just plain inept. When they handed out the fashion genes, I must have been in the ladies' room and missed out, like that actress at the Golden Globe awards a few years ago.

Hardly an occasion goes by when I don't commit some sort of fashion faux pas.

Last summer I went to a wedding where I made a special effort to look nice. I bought a long, flowing black skirt, white top, and shimmery sweater. Boy did I feel spiffy—until I got there and saw that all the other woman were wearing short little cocktail dresses, most of them strapless.

As I stepped through the door, I could hear an alarm go off and see the needle on the frump-o-meter swing all the way over.

I felt lower than a belly tick on a dog. I glanced around to find photographers from *People* Magazine. If they'd been handing out a prize for worst-dressed, I could have won it hands down.

My fashion sense is unerringly off. Name any occasion and I will wear the wrong outfit—guaranteed. And I'm a little too old to be calling up my friends and asking them what they're going to wear to the party.

I have the same problem with accessories. If by accident I happen to get the clothes right, you can count on me to add the wrong jewelry. If clunky is in, mine will be dainty. And if wide belts are in vogue, I'll be wearing them narrow.

Basically it comes down to this: If you want to be in style, wear the exact opposite of whatever I'm wearing. You can't go wrong.

I'm so out of sync that I've started embracing it as a talent. If you're stylistically incorrect all the time, you learn to compensate. Now when I arrive at a function and discover that I wore the wrong thing, I just figure it's my job to make everyone else feel better about themselves.

Others can look at me and think, "I'm not the only one who's chic challenged."

The fashion industry spends billions of dollars each year to keep me off balance. They change the styles just when I've bought something halfway trendy. My last decent outfit stayed in style for all of five minutes.

It's a conspiracy and I've finally figured it out.

Just as your daughter will not want to wear the wedding dress that you had hermitically sealed before she was born, you can rest assured that any classic clothes you've been saving will never, ever be in style again.

Let's face it: the plaid pants that looked bad in the 1970s still look bad. Even the retro look has been updated, so don't let anyone fool you into pulling out your original bell-bottoms.

People can always tell when you're trying too hard. Once I bought a nice sleeveless blouse for a camping trip, only to find everyone else wearing ratty T-shirts.

"This isn't a cruise," one gal snorted. I always suspected she was laughing at me, not with me.

My only hope for dressing success is to find a cardinal rule and stick to it.

As designer Vivienne Westwood advised, "When in doubt, overdress." ▼

SPIDER GUY

HE CAME TO my door with a clipboard in his hand and a somber expression on his face.

"Can I help you?" I asked.

"Ma'am, I'm here to talk to you about bugs," he said with a grave smile. This guy was more serious than a funeral director.

"I'll be happy to take a brochure if you have one," I said.

"Do you have pests?" he asked.

Only the ones that come to my front door, I thought.

Out loud I said, "We have ants and spiders. If you'd like to give me an estimate, I'll keep it on hand."

"I can't give you a quote until I see the extent of the problem," he said. "If you'll show me the way to your back gate, I'll just take a quick look around."

Which is how I found myself on an insect safari in the backyard with Spider Guy, who was earnestly examining the numerous points of entry into our house.

He pointed them all out—the ant trails, the spider webs, the cracks around the windows.

"We paint a product at the edge of your concrete where it meets the grass," he explained. "The ants carry it back to homes on their little feet, and 14 days later, their whole nest implodes."

I wondered if this guy had a military background.

He checked under the barbeque. "Here's where you'll see signs of rats."

"Usually I see them running across the back fence," I commented.

He lifted up the edge of each flower pot and trash can, then pointed to the door of our tool shed.

"And here's where we usually find *these*," he confided, tapping his index finger on a picture of a black widow spider.

I noticed he didn't use the actual words, black widow spider. It reminded me of the evil lord in Harry Potter, He Who Must Not Be Named—a name so horrible, it can't be spoken aloud.

"A bite from one of these spiders will kill anything that weighs less than 70 pounds," he said. "You and me—we'd get really sick. But something small, it would die."

I made a mental note to keep my body weight up, just in case.

He moved on and pointed to the eaves. "We'd sweep out all these spider egg sacks and come back in 30 days to destroy the next generation." He could sense victory right around the corner.

Then we sat down to talk about the cost. He pulled out a sheet with figures based on the square footage of the house. Just as I suspected: He could have quoted me a price without touring the yard.

"You have ants and spiders," he concluded. I always like a person who agrees with me.

He quoted a price that sounded plenty reasonable, especially when you think of all the dangers he'd be saving us from. I'd pay that much just for the peace of mind.

When I reported to my husband inside, he didn't think we needed it—this from a man who dozed through the whole spiel in the safety of his recliner.

I thanked Spider Guy, declined his services and went back inside. The first thing I saw on the table was a movie rental—*Charlotte's Web*.

Now there's a bit of irony for you. I had almost signed up for a service to wipe out all the little Charlottes around my house.

It was a close call. ▼

SENIOR BUFFET

EVERYONE LOVES A free sample. If you don't believe me, just check the aisles at Costco on any day between 11:00a.m. and 4:00p.m.

These are the prime snack-while-you-shop hours, the best time to visit what writer Janet Evanovich calls the "senior buffet." Like the characters in her books, I stop by Costco when I'm feeling a little hungry but am short on cash.

You can always tell when there's a tasty product about to be served. Like greedy crows on trash day, people hover in the aisles waiting to swoop in for the grab and gobble.

Sometimes the sample servers have to barricade the food to keep customers from snatching the snacks too soon.

Still, my Favorite Dotter aspires to the job.

"When I grow up, I want to be a greeter at Wal-Mart or give out samples at Costco," she said when she was younger. You have to admire a person who knows what she wants to do with her life.

Giving out samples is arguably one of the best jobs at Costco. And eating them is even better.

But it's not a free-for-all—there are rules. Parents must hand the samples to their kids. And you can't put it back once you touch it, for obvious reasons.

I've often wondered who decides which foods will be sampled on a particular day. Is there a dietician in charge? I suspect so, because last time I went, the menu was as varied as a five-course feast.

Starting in the front of the store with a taste of fruit crisps, I munched my way past the green salad with dressing, took a lap around the deli to taste the grilled sausage, tri-tip and angus burgers, then trotted by the cheesy baked potatoes and multi-grain bread. I finished in the back with a bite of frozen fudge bar for dessert.

All that was missing was the beverage to wash it all down. Luckily I carry my own water bottle.

It's also why I suspect there's a mastermind behind it all, somebody keeping an eye on the nutritional pyramid.

On a good day you've got all the major food groups. On a bad day, you get your choice of rug cleaner, chewable vitamins, and raw vegetable juice with onions. On those days I feel bad for the demonstrators. Crowds pass by without even making eye contact. It has to damage their self-esteem.

Sometimes you hit the jackpot with the hummus road show. Then you can pull over and try all 14 flavors on pita bread, while pretending to choose three kinds to buy.

Too bad the servers don't take requests. When I asked one demonstrator when I could sample the chocolate-covered pomegranate ice cream bars, she said, "I don't know, I just serve what they tell me."

I see—just following orders.

There is a limit to the store's generosity. I've noticed there are certain items they don't give out as samples. Can you picture them cutting up a shirt and giving a sleeve to one person and a collar to the next?

Or handing out pages one by one from the latest bestseller? There's a riot waiting to happen. "Hey, I wanted page 237."

And you never see a wine-tasting booth. There's probably a law against alcohol samples.

Conventional wisdom says never to shop when you're hungry. But when it's meal time, all roads lead to Costco.

Warning: this cart stops for snacks. ▼

BOOK CLUB

MY FIRST CLUE that it was a book group of teachers was when somebody said, "Raise your hand."

I guess I'd known from the outset that we were all educators, but I'd never actually heard someone say "Shhh" at a book club before.

Or, "Now get out your crayons and draw a picture of how you felt about the book."

Neither had I ever seen a toy elephant passed around as a signal for when it was your turn to talk—extra credit if you made an elephant sound before you started. One gal could only muster a weak whinny, but she was still allowed to speak. Other listeners showed their solidarity by raising one arm like a trunk and trumpeting loudly.

The book club's initial meeting was at happy hour, which turned out to be fitting metaphor for the entire evening.

One of the happier members kept hugging her book and repeating, "I really, really liked it." She'd had some experience reading elementary book reports, I could tell. And she was unwavering in her opinion each time the elephant came around.

When I told my husband that I was visiting a book club where the women liked to party more than they liked to discuss, he said, "Maybe they should start a magazine club." He was reading *People* magazine at the time, so you can see where his head was at.

I knew I was going to have a good time when my friend spoke in alliterated phrases on the way to the meeting. "I'm having a double-deodorant day," she divulged.

"Let me write that down," I said. "Can I use it in my column?"

After we arrived, one of the younger teachers spoke up. "I didn't want to come," she confessed, "because I thought we'd have to *learn* something."

Another poor soul hadn't finished the book. But to her credit, she didn't stick her fingers in her ears and sing "la-la-la-la-la," as I've been known to do when I don't want someone to ruin the ending.

Okay, I may have also done it in movie theaters during the previews.

As with many new book clubs, the topic of naming the group came up. Bodacious Babes was suggested, as well as the Cocktail Club, and Booktails —a clever combination of books and beverages.

Choosing the next book selection triggered a flurry of questions.

"Is there any smut?" asked one member.

"Does it have pictures?" inquired another.

"Do we have to read a chapter book?" whined a third.

The best book clubs have food, and this one was no exception. Thankfully, the hostess went with a menu unrelated to the circus theme of the book, *Water for Elephants*—which took place during prohibition days—so we were spared from eating cotton candy and sipping bootleg brandy.

Book clubs come in all shapes and sizes, with individual personalities of their own. I've been to one group where reading the classics was prescribed like a dose of medicine, nasty but necessary: "Let's read this book—it'll be good for us."

Other groups never get around to talking about the book at all. And some are so serious about wanting to party that they pay a professional to come in and lead the discussion.

Now that's my idea of the perfect job.

The best groups are the ones which combine friends and food with the love of books. That's why I've thought of starting my own book club.

Its name? Read 'em and Eat. ▼

ABOUT THE TYPE

This book was set in Garamond, a typeface originally designed by the Parisian type cutter, Claude Garamond, long before any of us were born. I chose this typeface because it was free.

For more about how frugal I am, see Volume 2, coming in 2015.

▼

ABOUT THE AUTHOR

Lois Swagerty lives in Carlsbad, California and Santa Fe, New Mexico. Her writing has appeared in *Today's Local News*, *Carlsbad Magazine*, *Costco Connection*, *Good News, Etc.*, Leadership Network publications and sometimes on the shower wall.

Visit her at www.loisswagerty.com.

▼

Made in the USA
San Bernardino, CA
18 November 2015